Mentoring for Young Peopl in Care and Leaving Care

Mentoring for Young People in Care and Leaving Care offers a rich exploration of the theory, research and practice relating to youth mentoring as a means of essential social support. Brady, Dolan and McGregor ground their work on the premise that the informal social support provided through a high-quality mentoring relationship can help young people in care to sustain positive mental health, cope with stress and fulfil their potential through adolescence and into adulthood.

It provides an up-to-date synthesis of research findings in relation to natural mentoring, formal mentoring and youth-initiated mentoring for children in care and explores the challenges and considerations relating to practice in this area. Illustrated with the details of original research with care-experienced young people, it offers much-needed insight into how young people interpret and make sense of their experiences in care and of mentoring.

Written to be accessible by those with limited knowledge of youth mentoring, this timely publication will be essential reading for academics, policy makers and practitioners in the fields of adolescent development, social care, social work and youth work.

Dr Bernadine Brady is a Lecturer and Senior Researcher at the UNESCO Child & Family Research Centre, NUI, Galway.

Professor Pat Dolan is Director of the UNESCO Child and Family Research Centre at NUI, Galway and holder of the UNESCO Chair in Children, Youth and Civic Engagement.

Professor Caroline McGregor is Professor at the School of Political Science and Sociology, NUI, Galway with lead responsibility for the discipline of social work. She is also a Senior Research Fellow at the UNESCO Child and Family Research Centre.

Adolescence and Society
Series Editor: John C. Coleman
Department of Education, University of Oxford

In the 20 years since it began, this series has published some of the key texts in the field of adolescent studies. The series has covered a very wide range of subjects, almost all of them being of central concern to students, researchers and practitioners. A mark of its success is that a number of books have gone to second and third editions, illustrating its popularity and reputation.

The primary aim of the series is to make accessible to the widest possible readership important and topical evidence relating to adolescent development. Much of this material is published in relatively inaccessible professional journals, and the objective of the books has been to summarise, review and place in context current work in the field, so as to interest and engage both an undergraduate and a professional audience.

The intention of the authors is to raise the profile of adolescent studies among professionals and in institutions of higher education. By publishing relatively short, readable books on topics of current interest to do with youth and society, the series makes people more aware of the relevance of the subject of adolescence to a wide range of social concerns.

The books do not put forward any one theoretical viewpoint. The authors outline the most prominent theories in the field and include a balanced and critical assessment of each of these. Whilst some of the books may have a clinical or applied slant, the majority concentrate on normal development.

The readership rests primarily in two major areas: the undergraduate market, particularly in the fields of psychology, sociology and education; and the professional training market, with particular emphasis on social work, clinical and educational psychology, counselling, youth work, nursing and teacher training.

Also in this series:

Mentoring for Young People in Care and Leaving Care
Bernadine Brady, Pat Dolan and Caroline McGregor

www.routledge.com/Adolescence-and-Society/book-series/SE0238

Mentoring for Young People in Care and Leaving Care
Theory, Policy and Practice

Bernadine Brady, Pat Dolan and Caroline McGregor

LONDON AND NEW YORK

First published 2020
by Routledge
2 Park Square, Milton Park, Abingdon, Oxon OX14 4RN

and by Routledge
52 Vanderbilt Avenue, New York, NY 10017

Routledge is an imprint of the Taylor & Francis Group, an informa business

© 2020 Bernadine Brady, Pat Dolan and Caroline McGregor

The right of Bernadine Brady, Pat Dolan and Caroline McGregor to be identified as authors of this work has been asserted by them in accordance with sections 77 and 78 of the Copyright, Designs and Patents Act 1988.

All rights reserved. No part of this book may be reprinted or reproduced or utilised in any form or by any electronic, mechanical, or other means, now known or hereafter invented, including photocopying and recording, or in any information storage or retrieval system, without permission in writing from the publishers.

Trademark notice: Product or corporate names may be trademarks or registered trademarks, and are used only for identification and explanation without intent to infringe.

British Library Cataloguing-in-Publication Data
A catalogue record for this book is available from the British Library

Library of Congress Cataloging-in-Publication Data
A catalog record for this book has been requested

ISBN: 978-1-138-55141-1 (hbk)
ISBN: 978-1-138-55143-5 (pbk)
ISBN: 978-1-315-14757-4 (ebk)

Typeset in Sabon
by Apex CoVantage LLC

Printed and bound by CPI Group (UK) Ltd, Croydon, CR0 4YY

Contents

	Acknowledgements	vii
1	Introduction and overview	1
2	Children in care and leaving care: issues and challenges	25
3	Natural and youth-initiated mentoring	43
4	Formal youth mentoring for children in care and leaving care	59
5	Introducing the current study	77
6	Young people's perspectives on the benefits of mentoring	93
7	Youth perspectives on relational dynamics and quality in mentoring relationships	119
8	Mentoring for young people in care: messages for policy and practice	135
	Index	151

Acknowledgements

The authors would like to offer their thanks to a number of people who contributed to this book in various ways. Special thanks to series editor, John Coleman and all the team at Routledge, particularly Charlotte Mapp and Lucy Kennedy who were a pleasure to work with at all stages of the process.

Our sincere thanks to all of the young people who took part in the study featured in this book and spoke so openly and eloquently about their experiences. We hope we have done you justice. Thanks also to the parents, carers and mentors who helped the young people to attend interviews. We would like to thank Sean Campbell and John Cahill, Foróige for facilitating us to undertake the research study, while a huge debt of gratitude is due to the staff of the Foróige Big Brothers Big Sisters Programme, especially Mary Lynch and Jill Murray, who worked closely with us on all aspects of the research. Thanks also to Brenda Keating, Sinead Murphy, Caroline Cronin, Louise Tuffy, Clodagh Rogers and Finghin McClafferty who provided invaluable assistance with recruitment, logistics and countless other issues. The study was greatly enriched by the valuable input of the members of the study advisory group – thank you to Jumoke, Vanessa and Ciara-Beth.

We would like to acknowledge the support of our colleagues at the UNESCO Child and Family Research Centre and the School of Political Science and Sociology, NUI Galway, particularly John Canavan, Gillian Browne and Emily O'Donnell. Thanks also to NUI Galway, for facilitating Bernadine to take sabbatical leave for during 2017-2018, during which much of this book was written. We would also like to thank Mike Hynes and all at the Social Science Research Centre, NUI Galway for the use of a quiet space to work on the manuscript. Thanks to Lisa Moran who offered valuable insights and advice and to Barbara Mircovic and Kayleigh Murphy for their assistance.

Bernadine Brady
Pat Dolan
Caroline McGregor
Galway 2019

1 Introduction and overview

1.1 Introduction

Research has shown that the needs of young people in care[1] are often complex and extensive because of the reasons for their admission to care and/or the challenges associated with being in care. While these needs often require formal supports, such as psychology or social work, there is increasing evidence that the availability of informal social support from a trusted adult can also make a significant difference in the lives of young people. Research has shown that many young people in care draw on natural mentors (i.e. non-parental adults) for guidance, encouragement and emotional support and that those who do so tend to experience more positive outcomes (Munson, Smalling, Spencer, Scott, & Tracy, 2010; Singer, Berzin, & Hokanson, 2013). However, these supportive relationships are often lacking for some young people in care; research has shown that many such young people feel that they lack personal, emotional and practical support from a trusted adult (Baker, 2017; Kersley & Estep, 2014).

Formal mentoring programmes aim to replicate the benefits of natural mentoring relationships by 'matching' a young person with a volunteer mentor who can be a friend and support to him or her. The youth mentoring model recognises that many young people prefer to look to an informal source for ongoing emotional support than to a professional helper, and value social connections that they perceive to be authentic, confidential and meaningful (Dolan & Brady, 2012). Mentoring can be considered a flexible intervention that is capable of working with the 'whole young person' in his or her own environment, culture, context and gender and building on their unique strengths. As a social policy intervention, mentoring also has the advantage of being available outside of 'working hours' and thus has the potential to provide support to young people when needed (Brady & Dolan, 2007).

While there is a growing body of research exploring the outcomes associated with natural and formal youth mentoring for children in care, there is currently no book that brings together theory, research and practice in relation to youth mentoring in a care context. This book aims to address this gap by providing a comprehensive synthesis of current international literature on theory and practice relating to mentoring for young people in care and leaving care. It also includes the findings of new qualitative research with young people in care regarding their experiences of formal mentoring and how it impacted on their lives.

In this opening chapter, the authors set out the context for this volume and introduce the key rationale and concepts of the book. The reader is provided with a brief introduction to the nature of adolescent development, with consideration of the challenges which some young people can face during their transition from childhood to adulthood. The concept of children and youth living in or leaving care is introduced and key issues highlighted. Some of the key theoretical perspectives on mentoring are considered; including social support, coping, resilience, relational cultural theory and social capital. Finally, an outline of the structure and content of the book that follows this introductory chapter is provided.

1.2 Adolescence

Described as the journey from childhood to adulthood, adolescence is a time of rapid development and change. These changes, which generally start at around 12 years of age include bursts of physical growth coupled with processes of emotional regulation and cognitive or intellectual development. This process of adolescent development is often described in terms of transitions (Feldman & Elliot, 1990; Coleman & Hendry, 1999). Though the concept of adolescence as a time of 'storm and stress' has been challenged, commentators agree that few developmental periods are characterised by so many physical, social and psychological changes as adolescence. Drawing on the work of developmental theorists such as Erickson (1968), Eccles and Gootman (2002, p. 48) summarise the challenges faced by adolescents as follows:

- Changing the nature of the relationship between young people and their parents
- Exploring new personal, social and sexual roles and identities
- Transforming peer relationships into deeper friendships and intimate partnerships
- Participating in a series of experiences and choices that facilitate future economic independence

These changes take place in complex social settings and are dependent upon the assets of the individual, the social supports available to them and the developmental appropriateness of the settings encountered by young people as they pass through adolescence (Eccles & Gootman, 2002). A large body of research underlines the role of the parents and family in providing a stable foundation for healthy development into adulthood (Bowlby, 1953; Erickson, 1968). The social environment in which the family live is also important – according to Seden (2002, p. 195), child development is 'a complex interaction of the individual, the adults who determine the child's upbringing and the social environment'. Most young people draw upon the supports of family, school and community to make the transition to adulthood without serious difficulty. A minority of young people experience difficulties, however, particularly where there is stress in the family and social environment. For young people who experience adversity, adolescence can be a particularly troubled and tumultuous period (Rutter, 2012).

While the social context of the youth phase is always changing, it can be argued that the nature of youth transitions to adulthood has been particularly affected by the intense social change that has occurred in recent decades (Cote, 2014). Children are increasingly likely to grow up in a lone or step-parent family, while the collective security traditionally provided by church and community has declined. Everyday life has become increasingly mediated by technology and social media, bringing greater exposure to marketing and consumerism and an expectation of constant social engagement. Young people have the freedom to question established beliefs and certainties, can enjoy a plurality of identities and lifestyles and are expected to be reflexive and proactive about their futures (Farrugia, 2013; Furlong, 2013). While liberating in many ways, a consequence of these changes is that people can experience self-doubt, anxiety and depression in the face of an infinite range of possibilities (Farrugia, 2013).

1.3 Young people in care and leaving care

The term 'in care' is used to refer to young people living in or 'looked after' in alternative care, which are public-welfare supported arrangements, or private arrangements coming under statutory control, for children living out of their own homes. While there are a broad range of types of alternative care, the most common forms are foster care (family based) and residential care (institution or group) settings. In addition to these formal models of care, many children are looked after in informal kinship care arrangements by relatives or friends. Children generally enter into alternative care due to reasons such as death of a parent or parents, neglect, abuse or the inability of their parents to care for them for reasons that may include addiction, disability or acute poverty.

For some children, coming into care can be a positive experience, offering a sanctuary from abuse and harm, while for others it can be profoundly difficult experience, where they feel wrenched from the familiarity and comfort of family and community. Many children experience emotions and difficulties related to separation, loss, attachment, trauma and bereavement as a result of their experiences (Healey & Fisher, 2011). The effects of these experiences can have implications for the child's adjustment to life in care and their ability to form attachments with other adults. Depending on the timing and circumstances of entry into care, being in care may involve moving away from home, changes of school, having to make new friends and adjusting to a new environment, while the child must take on a dual or multiple identity as a member of their birth family and foster family (McMahon & Curtin, 2013). When relationships and placements are disrupted, the young person must repeatedly 'start over' and can fall behind at school. Furthermore, young people may feel embarrassed or stigmatised about their care experience and struggle with the ongoing presence of social care professionals in their lives (Sutton & Stack, 2012; Selwyn & Riley, 2015). Young people in care must learn to cope with these experiences in addition to the normative pressures of adolescence.

While many children thrive in care and do very well, the general trend observed in research is that outcomes in relation to education, health and well-being tend to be relatively poorer for children in care (Baker, Briheim-Crookall, Magnus, & Selwyn, 2019; Stein, 2012; Stein & Munro, 2008; Gypen, Vanderfaeillie, De Maeyer, Belenger, & Van Holen, 2017). When the time comes to leave care at age 18, young people must also adapt quickly to independent life in comparison to their peers who can rely on more extensive family support into adulthood. Empirical studies in a range of countries have attested to the challenges faced by young people transitioning from care, particularly when these transitions are fractured, accelerated and poorly supported (Carr & Mayock, 2019).

However, decades of research have also shown that outcomes are better where the young person has positive resources in his or her life, such as stability and continuity of care, strong relationships, professional support and personal motivation. A key theme in research on outcomes is the importance of supporting relationships and maintaining continuity in the lives of young people in care and leaving care (Baker, 2017; Fahlberg, 2012; Stein, 2012). Those involved in supporting young people in care can play a key role in increasing the chances for successful outcomes. In recent years, greater emphasis is placed on the importance of relationships in social work generally, and child protection specifically (Hingley-Jones & Ruch, 2016). This welcome refocus strengthens support for considering how relationships-oriented work can be developed within formal systems of support – especially when it comes to working with children and young people (Winter et al., 2016). The importance of avoiding a narrow focus on 'child protection' in interventions is also emphasised in recent literature (Parton, 2014b; Devaney & McGregor, forthcoming).

While access to a range of formal agency supports through social work, specialist mental health, educational and welfare services is essential to support children in care as required, sometimes this is not sufficient even with the increased emphasis on relationship based practices. As we discuss in more detail especially in Chapter 8, there are many complex reasons why reliance on the social worker/professional relationship alone will be insufficient for meeting the needs of the young person. Even in cases where relationships are strong between young people and their professional support workers, young people also need robust and dependable informal support systems. While foster parents, family, friends and community members provide invaluable informal social support for many, some young people in care do not have such supportive relationships in their lives (Baker, 2017). As we will discuss in more detail as the book progresses, there is considerable potential for professional support services to support and encourage the formation of mentoring relationships for young people in care. Research has found that mentors can enhance the informal support system of the young person, both through the relationship directly and by connecting the young person with social opportunities through which they can develop friendship and support networks. While it is important to caution that mentoring will not be appropriate or required for every young person and should not be seen as a 'panacea', McGregor, Lynch, and Brady (2017, p. 355) argue that the potential offered by this approach is not being realised at present, with social services perhaps relying too much on formal services only.

1.4 Youth mentoring

Youth mentoring can be understood as a caring, trusting and supportive relationship between a young person and a non-parental figure who provides guidance, support and encouragement to the mentee (Schwartz, Lowe, & Rhodes, 2012; Rhodes, Spencer, Keller, Liang, & Noam, 2006). Mentoring can have an impact on young people by enhancing social and emotional well-being, improving cognitive skills and promoting positive identity development through role modelling and advocacy (Rhodes et al., 2006). Research has shown that mentored young people can have positive gains in many aspects of their lives, including social, emotional, behavioural and academic domains (Spencer, 2012).

Mentoring has a long history and can be found in ancient cultures and folklore. The Greek mythological story *The Odyssey* has the first description and mention of the term Mentor (meaning wise one). Mentor was a support and guide to Telemachus in what was probably the first recorded youth mentoring match, albeit a mythological one (Online Etymology Dictionary, 2018). In Irish folklore, mentoring features in the fabled life story of the mythical Fionn macCumhal, an ancient Irish warrior and folk hero who was leader of the Fianna, a prominent Irish tribe. Orphaned at a young age, Fionn was mentored by the bard Finnegas. Finnegas, who was an unofficial meantóir (Irish word for mentor) to Fionn, taught general wisdom as well as the art of poetry (MacLeoid & MacWilliam, 1989).

Mentor and Finnegas can be seen as *natural or informal mentors,* non-parental adults, such as extended family members, neighbours, teachers and coaches from whom a young person receives support and guidance (Horn & Spencer, 2018, p. 183). These relationships develop organically within the young person's social network and are maintained by the youth and adult involved, without external intervention. Research has found that many young people identify the presence of a natural mentor in their lives and that such mentors can provide support, act as role models, encourage learning and skills development, promote self-esteem and connect young people with opportunities (Southwick, Morgan, Vythilingam, & Charney, 2007; Stanton-Salazar, 2011). The results of a meta-analytic review of 30 studies of natural mentoring conducted since 1992 (Van Dam et al., 2018) found that the presence of a natural mentor was associated with positive youth outcomes, particularly in the areas of social-emotional development and academic and vocational achievement.

Because not all young people have natural mentors in their lives but may benefit from having such a relationship, *formal mentoring* programmes have been established to facilitate the formation of mentoring relationships between volunteer non-parental adults and young people. In essence, formal mentoring refers to the process of matching mentors with young people who need or want a caring, responsible adult in their lives. Overall the aim of mentoring relationships is to create 'a supportive social bond between a young person and an adult in which trust and closeness can develop and the adult can help the young person to cope and develop to the best of his or her abilities' (Dolan & Brady, 2012, p. 128). Clayden and Stein (2005) highlight that mentoring programmes can be targeted at outcomes that are either 'instrumental' (i.e. focused on outcomes such as employment, education or training) or 'expressive' – focused on 'soft' outcomes, such as personal development. While developing a one-to-one relationship between mentor and mentee is the main focus for the intervention, many mentoring programmes also aim to support the social integration of the young person into wider environment and social settings in which they live.

While youth mentoring has been in existence for over a century in the United States, there has been a strong growth in youth mentoring programmes both in the United States and worldwide over the past three decades (Matz, 2013; Preston, Prieto-Flores, & Rhodes, 2018). Youth mentoring programmes are frequently suggested as a policy response to a range of social issues. In the United Kingdom, mentoring was integrated into a range of government policy initiatives aimed at reducing social exclusion among children, young people and families from the 1990s onwards (Colley, 2003; Philip & Spratt, 2007). Preston et al. (2018) argue that concerns about inequality and delinquency have been major drivers of program expansion in the United States, while in continental Europe, the desire to support immigrant young people to develop community bonds and to realise their potential in the education system has been a significant influence on the growth of mentoring programmes in recent years (Prieto-Flores, Feu, & Casademont, 2016).

Research has shown that youth mentoring programmes can be successful in enhancing emotional and psychological well-being among young people, with studies reporting outcomes including greater life satisfaction, hopefulness and reduced anxiety and depression (Barry, Clarke,

Morreale, & Field, 2018; Cavell & Elledge, 2014; Dolan et al., 2011). Studies have also reported improved social relationships and skills (De Wit, DuBois, Erdem, Larose, & Lipman, 2016; DuBois, Holloway, Valentine, & Cooper, 2002), reductions in problem behaviour, including aggression and substance abuse (Tolan, Henry, Schoeny, Lovegrove, & Nichols, 2014) and improved educational outcomes, including staying in education for longer, better school attendance and better academic grades (Herrera, Grossman, Kauh, Feldman, & McMaken, 2007; Matz, 2013; Simões & Alarcão, 2014). Mentoring programmes are more likely to achieve positive outcomes if they implement evidence-based program practices, including careful screening and matching of mentors and mentees, training and ongoing support for mentors and having expectations for frequent meeting (Kupersmidt, Stump, Stelter, & Rhodes, 2017; Raposa, Ben-Eliyahu, Olsho, & Rhodes, 2019).

While mentoring programmes can be provided in schools, online or other settings, the model referred to in this book is that of one-to-one community-based mentoring. Community-based mentoring programmes typically recruit and train adult volunteers and match them with young people who are deemed to benefit from a relationship with a non-parental adult. While expectations vary according to the programme type, the mentoring pair is expected to meet weekly for a year or more. During this time, the 'match' is supported by caseworkers from the mentoring programme who ensure that both the young person and mentor are satisfied with the relationship and assist in troubleshooting if any problems arise. Many youth mentoring programmes are run by voluntary organisations in the community but work closely with statutory social services. Community based mentoring can take the form of a stand-alone intervention or may be part of a wider youth work programme. Stein (2012) argues that mentoring can be seen as occupying a space between professional social services and informal support from family and friends.

In recent years, a new form of mentoring has emerged that brings together aspects of formal and natural mentoring, called *youth-initiated mentoring*. Rather than being assigned a mentor, young people are supported to recruit caring adults from within their own networks (e.g. relative, neighbour or friend). As with formal mentoring programmes, support for the mentoring relationship, including goal setting and troubleshooting, is provided by a mentoring organisation or other social care professionals. By recruiting a mentor from the young person's own social network, it is envisaged that the mentoring relationship will develop more quickly, be more sustainable in the long term than one created through a formal mentoring programme and ensure it is someone that the young person can identify with (Spencer, Tugenberg, Ocean, Schwartz, & Rhodes, 2016).

1.5 Youth mentoring for children in care

Over the past decade in particular, there has been an increased focus on research exploring the benefits of natural and formal mentoring for children in care. In

Chapter 3, we synthesise the findings of research in relation to natural mentoring for children in care. The evidence indicates that natural mentors play an important role in the lives of many children and young people in care, and that many studies reported a positive relationship between natural mentoring and improved psychosocial, behavioural or academic outcomes (Ahrens, DuBois, Richardson, Fan, & Lozano, 2008; Duke, Farruggia, & Germo, 2017; Munson & McMillen, 2009; Thompson, Greeson, & Brunsink, 2016). Research has also shown that young people prefer mentors who are non-judgemental, authentic and there when needed. Young people value mentors who have had similar life experiences to them, particularly those that have had some experience of the care system, while adults they had met through the child welfare system (such as social care workers or residential care staff) were also frequently valued as mentors (Ahrens et al., 2011; Munson et al., 2010). Because young people in care have often had many placement moves in their lives, having a consistent long-term relationship to support the young person through the multiple adversities and transitions that they faced in their lives was particularly valued (Munson et al., 2010). However, the potential for a consistent relationship of this nature to develop and be maintained is often challenged by the nature of life in care, whereby frequent disruption and changes of placement means that some young people in care can face difficulties in establishing or maintaining their relationships (Horn & Spencer, 2018). Emotional barriers to the formation of natural mentoring relationships were also identified in research, with some young people speaking of their fears that they would get hurt if they became close to the mentor and/or that the mentor would fail them in some way (Munson et al., 2010).

As we will see in Chapter 4, formal youth mentoring programmes for children and young people in care can take a number of different forms. They may be general mentoring programmes, which include children and young people in care as part of their target group or they may be enhanced or intensive approaches to mentoring for children in care. For example, Johnson, Pryce, and Martinovich (2011) found that a therapeutic mentoring programme was perceived to be beneficial in helping to reduce trauma symptoms in foster youth. A number of studies have reported on programmes providing mentoring for young people leaving care. Clayden and Stein (2005) found that voluntary mentors were seen by young people to offer a different type of relationship to those provided by professionals or by family members. Mentors were seen to provide practical assistance, such as advice in relation to accommodation, education, employment and training as well as emotional support, including listening and helping with relationship problems. Young people valued the mentoring relationship for building confidence and improving their emotional well-being.

Issues and challenges associated with youth mentoring for children in care

While youth mentoring can result in positive benefits for youth, it is important to note that it is not required nor does it work for every young person.

A key issue of concern with regard to formal mentoring for young people in care is that young people who have experienced abuse or maltreatment may experience attachment issues which make it more challenging for them to form close mentoring relationships or which may cause relationships to end early (Rhodes, 2005). Research has shown that when mentoring relationships close early or unexpectedly, youth may be at increased risk of experiencing harmful behavioural, emotional or social outcomes (Kupersmidt et al., 2017). Furthermore, the transient and changing nature of young people's lives may make it more difficult for a mentor to keep in touch and to 'gain a foothold' in the life of the young person. There is also evidence that some young people don't feel comfortable accessing the support of a mentor through a formal programme, with some preferring naturally occurring forms of support. In terms of programme related challenges, difficulties in the recruitment of suitable volunteers mean that young people often have to wait for considerable periods before being matched (Spencer, Gowdy, Drew, & Rhodes, 2019). These issues will be explored in greater detail throughout the book.

1.6 Youth mentoring: theoretical basis

There are a range of theoretical perspectives than can be drawn on to explain and justify considering youth mentoring as an intervention for young people in care. In this section, we review a selection of perspectives that have relevance in terms of children in care. Jean Rhodes's model of youth mentoring was developed specifically to explicate the processes by which youth mentoring impacts on youth. Other theories reviewed include social support, coping, resilience, relational cultural theory and social capital.

Rhodes model of youth mentoring

One of the most widely accepted theories of the youth mentoring process was developed by Jean Rhodes (2005). For Rhodes (2005, p. 31), a 'strong inter-personal connection, characterized by mutuality, trust and empathy' is a foundation from which a mentoring relationship can influence the social, emotional, identity and cognitive development of the young person.

According to Rhodes (2005), positive outcomes only become possible if a meaningful relationship develops between the mentor and mentee. The starting point of Rhodes's theoretical model, therefore, is the need for a 'strong inter-personal connection, characterized by mutuality, trust and empathy' (p. 31) (see Figure 1.1). If a close bond forms, the relationship can influence the young person in the following ways:

> *Social and emotional development:* Rhodes suggests that mentors may help young people to better understand and manage their positive and negative emotions. The relationship may provide a secure base from which the youth can negotiate adolescence and achieve crucial social

10 *Introduction and overview*

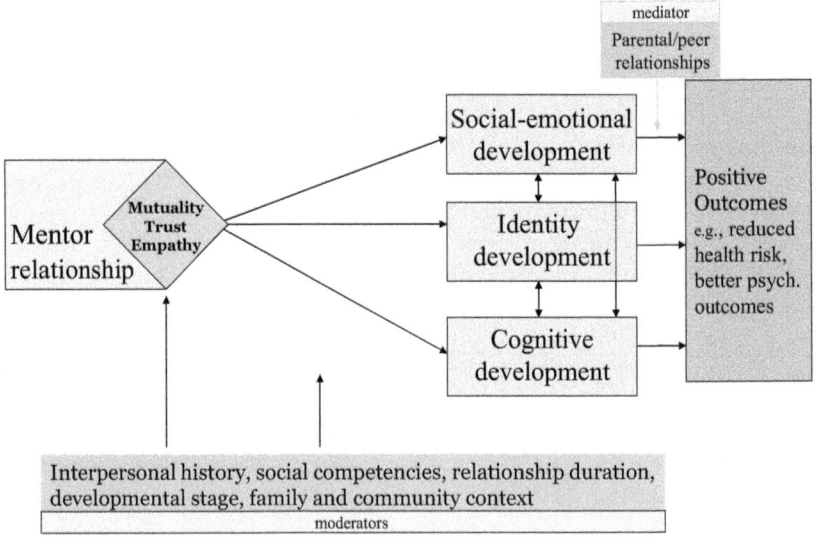

Figure 1.1 Pathways of mentoring influence
Source: Rhodes 2005

and cognitive competencies, while mentors may help the young person to form healthy relationships with others. The mentor can 'model' positive behaviour, demonstrating to the young person that positive relationships with adults are possible.

Cognitive development: Social interaction plays a major role in cognitive development processes. Developmental theorists argue that children or adolescents' interactions with caring adults 'stretch' their ability beyond what it would be if they acted alone, leading to the acquisition and refinement of new thinking skills. Meaningful, youth-relevant conversations can be a mechanism through which this happens. Rhodes suggests that mentoring can be a safe haven for youth to air sensitive issues and adults to offer advice (Rhodes, 2005).

Identity Development: Theorists such as Cooley (1902), Freud (1914), Mead (1934) and Erickson (1968) have argued that people's sense of self is influenced by the attitudes, behaviours and traits of people they wish to emulate. The mentoring process may influence the child's conception of his or her current and future identity.

Rhodes suggests that these factors work in tandem to influence the development of the young person in the mentoring relationship and can lead to positive outcomes, including reduced health risk and better psychological outcomes. According to Rhodes, Grossman, and Resch (2000), mentoring relationships can also alleviate some of the tensions and conflicts that arise in parent-child relationships during adolescence by helping the young person to deal with everyday stressors, providing a model for effective conflict resolution and indirectly reducing parental stress. In addition, a mentor's positive influence may improve the mentee's capacity to manage friendships and deal with problems that arise with peers (Rhodes, Haight, & Briggs, 1999). The outcomes accruing from the mentoring relationship may be mediated through improvements in these relationships.

Rhodes (2005) also draws our attention to a range of factors that may moderate the degree to which social, cognitive or identity development occurs through the mentoring relationship. Because mentoring is a process with a relationship at its core, the young person's attachment status might moderate the effects of mentoring. Children with a history of good relationships may find it easier to form a bond with another adult and may use the mentoring relationship more for the acquisition of skills and critical thinking than for an emotional bond. Conversely, those who have experienced less secure relationships may initially be resistant but eventually develop a more intense bond with their mentor to help satisfy their social and emotional needs. The young person's social competencies, developmental stage, family and community context and the duration of the relationship are also likely to affect the mentoring processes (Rhodes, 2005).

Social support

Pilisuk and Parks (1981, p. 122) define social support as 'a range of interpersonal exchanges that include not only the provision of physical assistance, emotional caring, and information, but also the subjective consequence of making individuals feel that they are the object of enduring concerns by others'. Cassel (1976) found that a lack of social connectedness had negative effects on health and well-being, particularly during periods of high stress but that close protective social support networks could protect or 'buffer' people from the effects of such stress. He argues that it is optimal to strengthen social supports rather than to try to reduce exposure to stressors. The importance of support enlistment through solid social network sources of help during adolescence has been well identified (Cutrona, 2000). It has been found that adolescents who have experienced stressful events recover better if they feel they have good social support (Bal, Crombez, Van Oost, & Debourdeaudhuij, 2003).

For most young people, social support is a naturally occurring process, whereby a young person accesses and provides support in everyday life from their natural social networks including parents and siblings, extended family friendships, neighbours, sports coaches and teachers as well as other community contacts. These are the people to whom young people turn to first when they face a problem. Most typically, youth access different forms of assistance, including tangible or practical help, emotional support and compassion and/or advice and guidance (Dolan & Brady, 2012). The perceived quality of the support available is also critical; young people prefer helpers to whom they feel close and who are reliable, honest, genuine and non-demeaning (Bolger & Amarel, 2007). It is equally important that the young person is not just a recipient of help but reciprocates support in some way.

It has been found that people benefit from having different types of supporters in their networks (Cutrona, 2000). For example, they may draw on the support of a professional for expertise in addressing a particular issue, from a friend who is going through the same experience as them and from an uncle who can provide a listening ear or help out in practical ways. Additionally, the young person may benefit from the help of a 'veteran' that is someone who has gone through a similar stress and managed to cope and can share insights about his or her experience with them. At times of crisis, young people may access different types of support compared to their everyday living needs. For example, extended family members who might not provide day-to-day support may come to the fore during a particular crisis, for example, at times of bereavement. Furthermore, research has shown that perceived support – in other words, the help that a young person believes to be available to him – may be as important as support actually received (Bolger & Amarel, 2007). Cohen and Wills (1985) reviewed 40 studies and found consistent evidence that the perception that others are there for support is the key to stress buffering. Therefore, a belief that another person would offer support if needed retains value for a young person regardless of whether the support is accessed.

Research has found that young people in care and leaving care may have variability in the social support available to them. Some foster youth have a more difficult experience when transitioning from care due to a lack of strong familial and social support networks on which to rely. For example, Singer et al. (2013) explored the types of relationships experienced by young people who had left the foster care system and also the quality of these relationships from the young person's perspective. They found that while young people did identify a wide range of both informal and formal support during their transition to adulthood, there were 'holes' in the form of support, especially advice and practical support. Furthermore, it has been found that some young people leaving care can view independence as 'success' and may underestimate their need for supportive relationships or see such relationships as a sign of weakness (Greeson, Garcia, Kim, Thompson, & Courtney, 2015; Samuels & Pryce, 2008). Samuels and Pryce (2008) have called for a focus on 'interdependent living' rather than 'independent living' to emphasise the importance of supportive relationships in the transition to adulthood.

Coping

Whereas the research community has given much attention to understanding the factors that enable youth to thrive during the phases of early, middle and late adolescence (Santrock, 2012), less attention has been paid to the importance of their capacity to cope in family, school or community settings (Cotterell, 2007). It could be argued that a greater focus on adolescent coping has emerged in recent decades as a result of trends such as higher rates of self-harm and suicide among youth, youth unemployment, bullying and ever-increasing pressure on young people to do well in school. (Smokowski & Holland Kopasz, 2005).

Coping is defined by Frydenberg (2019) as 'behavioural and cognitive efforts used by individuals to manage the demands of a personal-environment relationship' (p. 26). Individuals' ability to cope is influenced by the available resources and their coping styles and strategies. While there is no right or wrong way to cope, some strategies have been labelled as 'productive' and others as 'non-productive'. Frydenberg (2019) identifies non-productive coping strategies among adolescents as including withdrawal, anger, disengagement from school and engagement in risk behaviour, while productive coping includes dealing with problems, anger management and taking part in recreation or hobbies. Previous studies have shown that productive coping is associated with higher levels of emotional well-being while non-productive coping is associated with lower levels of emotional wellbeing and depression (McKenzie & Frydenberg, 2004; Frydenberg, 2019). For Frydenberg (2019) coping is closely related to the concept of resilience, which can be best construed as an outcome of coping.

Family is a key resource for adolescents but research has shown that family stress, parenting and resources impact negatively on productive coping strategies. It is likely, therefore, that the coping resources of children in care have been undermined by the difficulties that they have experienced in their family lives. A study by McKenzie and Frydenberg (2004) with young people in Australia found that young people high in familial resources tended to use productive coping strategies, whereas those with fewer resources tended to use more non-productive strategies. Frydenberg (2019) argues that a focus on building up young people's resources, such as healthy interpersonal relationships, is required alongside the development of coping skills. When discussing the findings of our primary research in Chapter 6, we draw on these theoretical perspectives to argue that youth mentoring relationships can support young people in care to cope more effectively with the challenges faced in their lives.

Resilience

As noted earlier, young people in care can experience significant adversities in their lives, including family breakdown, abuse, mental health problems and poverty. Whereas in the past the pathways by which young people can overcome such serious difficulties were to some extent unknown, the concept of adolescence resilience or the capacity for a young person to bounce back and do well is now prominent in the literature and within youth work and welfare practices across a range of disciplines (Rutter, 2012). The term *resilience*, which comes from the Latin 'il satire', has been described as thriving in the face of adversity, bouncing back and doing better than expected and requires two conditions. Firstly, for any young person to be described as being resilient, he or she needs to be or have faced adversity in his or her life. Secondly, the young person must not just cope with but actually thrive in spite of the adversity experienced.

Ann Masten's extensive work on resilience in children highlights the importance of the 'everyday magic' or mundane and regular support from others including family and friends as a key component of resilience (Masten, 2004). Alternatively some think of resilience as triggered by low points or critical moments which represent the start of recovery and thriving (Clarke & Clarke, 2003). Either way, the role of a significant supportive other adult or friend who provides unconditional support when needed can be a key resilience builder for youth. Edith Grotberg (1995) stressed the importance of not seeing resilience as inherent in the young person and his or her own agency only, but something that the young person's wider social ecology, including family, school, community and indeed social policy and civic society, has a role to play in (Liebenberg & Ungar, 2009).

Resilience is also often described in terms of young persons having risk and protective factors in their lives (Masten, 2004). Protective factors which are key to a young person thriving can include access to education and health care, secure housing, economic stability, social support and connectedness to family, friends and neighbourhoods and affiliation with community including religious or faith groups and positive arts and leisure pursuits (Garmezy, 1993). Most simply, Masten argues that where the protective factors outweigh the risk factors the young person is better equipped to demonstrate resilience. Social care professionals can help young people to be resilient by building connections to caring adults, increasing family and community belonging, enabling self-regulation skills, increasing positive motivation and thereby supporting the young person to have a positive view of self. The capacity of mentors to support the resilience of young people in care is considered throughout this book.

Relational cultural theory

While obvious, is important nonetheless to state that a human relationship is the key mechanism through which the mentoring process operates. Relational cultural theory (RCT) is a theoretical perspective which focuses on the power of positive social relationships. Proponents of RCT posit that meaningful relationships with others throughout the life-course are critical for psychological health and well-being. Because we as humans are 'hard-wired to connect', positive relationships characterised by empathy, mutuality and inter-dependence are essential. According to Jordan (2013), RCT is based on the belief that all psychological growth occurs in relationships and when people move out of relationships and into isolation, it results in psychological suffering. Miller (2008) identified five key outcomes from relational connections:

- Both parties feel a greater sense of energy as a result of their relationship
- As a result of being active in the world, both parties feel more capable of acting within the world and do so
- Participating in the relationship provides each person with a greater sense of self as well as a greater sense of the other
- Connections lead to a greater sense of self-worth
- People in connected relationships are motivated to seek out connections with others

(Horn & Spencer, 2018)

Many young people in care will have experienced disconnections in their relationships with others, which, according to Miller (2008), cause individuals to feel less energetic, to doubt their self-worth and to feel less inclined to seek new connections with others. These disconnections 'if left unrepaired, can lead to feelings of isolation and cause feelings of shame within the self, leading to a belief that one is unworthy and unvalued' (Horn & Spencer, 2018, p. 223). Where the young person has the opportunity to re-establish meaningful connection with others, they start to feel understood and less alone, helping them to move away from isolation (Jordan, 2013).

RCT is increasingly being seen as a useful theoretical perspective with which to understand why mentoring relationships can be important (Fletcher & Ragins, 2007; Buehler, 2017; Horn & Spencer, 2018; Ragins, 2012). Ragins (Fletcher & Ragins, 2007, p. 375) uses the term 'relational mentoring', to refer to two-sided, reciprocal relationships that involve mutual learning and influence, ultimately leading to outcomes that 'reflect the ability to operate effectively in a context of interdependence and connection'. In these types of mentoring relationships, the mentor does not have 'power over' but exercises 'power with' and 'power for' the mentee. In such relationships, both mentor and mentee contribute to one another and the relationship and all people grow as a result of their interactions. Jordan (2013) presents a model known as 'relational resilience', suggesting that that resilience resides not in the individual but in the capacity for connection to others through growth-fostering relationships.

Social capital

The term *social capital* is used to describe the resources provided by relationships, which aid in individuals' growth and adjustment (Duke et al., 2017). Bonding social capital refers to ties that are often close, durable and strong on emotional support, while bridging social capital is characterised by weak ties with people who are not close but which may be beneficial in terms of their personal or career progression (Putnam, 2000). Krauss (2019) further identifies three types of social connections or social capital that young people need in their lives. Firstly, there are 'lifelines', described as 'people who have your back no matter what'. These connections can be seen to provide emotional support and bonding social capital. Secondly, 'door openers' are people who introduce or integrate you into their own networks and groups, giving access to new social and economic advantages. Thirdly, 'navigators' are people we know who help us to 'play the game', for example, figuring out how an education, employment or other opportunity works. Krauss (2019) argues that young people from disadvantaged backgrounds may not realise they lack the kinds of social capital their more advantaged peers can easily access. Interventions are required 'to make sure they enter adulthood with the kinds of social currency they really need to succeed'.

It has been found that many young people leave care with 'social capital deficits' (Avery & Freundlich, 2009; Duke et al., 2017). It can be argued that mentoring aims to provide these types of connections or social capital, providing a trusting, supportive relationship between a young person and adult, and potentially opening up their social networks and worldviews and providing opportunities. Mentees often have the opportunity to take part in new activities, including sport, cultural and youth groups that otherwise may not be part of their worlds. Research on youth mentoring has provided many examples of ways in which social capital has been facilitated by mentors. Shildrick and MacDonald (2006) found that natural mentors facilitated young people to broaden their options and enjoy new lifestyles, while Clayden and Stein's (2005) study of mentoring for young people leaving care showed that informal relationships with mentors acted, in some cases, to support young people to bypass the negative bonding social capital that may otherwise have led them to engage in crime and drug use. Duke et al. (2017) found that youth depended heavily on natural mentors (or VIPs) to help fill those gaps in support and social capital normally afforded by a stable home environment.

1.7 Structure of the book

Following this introductory chapter, Chapter 2 considers the issues and challenges children in care and leaving care may face. The range of themes includes an emphasis on the diversity of care experiences over the life course, the importance of coping and the problem of stigma. We also discuss research on outcomes in key areas of life including education, mental health, well-being and behaviour.

Chapter 3 provides an overview of research evidence relating to natural mentoring for children in care with a focus on prevalence, key characteristics, challenges and practice implications. In this chapter, the concept of youth initiated mentoring is also explored, which involves supporting young people to seek out and recruit their own natural mentors in their social network.

In Chapter 4, the focus moves to formal mentoring. The first part of the chapter explores the research evidence in relation to youth mentoring in general, with its use for children in care specifically under scrutiny in the second part of the chapter. Research is reviewed in relation to outcomes for children in care taking part in general mentoring programmes and in intensive mentoring for young people with higher levels of need or risk and special projects aimed at youth mentoring for children in care and those transitioning out of care. The practice considerations and challenges involved in formal youth mentoring for young people in care are reviewed.

Chapter 5 will provide an overview of the study central to this reader and from which the primary data presented in the Chapters 6 and 7 is drawn. The Irish context for the study is described while the policy and legislative context in relation to child welfare in Ireland is outlined. The programmatic context for the study (Big Brothers Big Sisters Programme Ireland managed by Foróige) and research methodology, including ethical considerations, are described. We will see that the study aims to understand young people's subjective experiences of the mentoring relationship in the context of their overall lives. Detailed one-to-one narrative interviews were conducted with 13 young people who are currently or were previously participants in the BBBS youth mentoring programme while in care regarding their experiences of youth mentoring.

In Chapters 6 and 7, the emphasis moves towards telling the stories of participants about their experiences of mentoring and its meaning in the context of their overall lives. In Chapter 6, the findings from qualitative research with 13 young people regarding the benefits that they associated with mentoring in their lives are outlined. The mentoring relationship was seen to influence the social and emotional well-being of the young people in a range of ways including providing a social outlet, providing a listening ear, relieving stress and improving sociability and self-confidence. Mentors were also seen to support young people in terms of educational engagement, in the development of social capital and in processes of identity development. Chapter 7 focuses on young people's views on the characteristics of their mentors and of the mentoring relationship and their perspectives on how it differed to their other relationships within their social network, particularly family, friends and social workers. Chapter 8 brings together the key messages from the volume and provides guidance for future policy and practice related to mentoring for young people in care.

1.8 Conclusion

The chapter has introduced youth mentoring and explored its relevance to children and young people in care. A core assumption of the book is that both formal and informal support systems are essential for young people in care and that many young people benefit from having supportive adult (non-parental) relationships in their lives. A brief sketch of the theoretical rationale for youth mentoring is provided, incorporating Jean Rhodes's model of mentoring (2005), social support, coping, resilience, relational cultural theory and social capital. A more in-depth examination of the lived experiences of youth in care and leaving care will follow in Chapter 2.

Summary points: introduction and overview

- Adolescence can be a challenging time for young people, one that can be intensified for children in care.
- Youth mentoring can arise from natural or formal mentor relationships.
- Although formal services like social work are increasingly aware of the importance of relationships, young people in care also need other natural forms of support within their own social networks.
- A number of theories relating to coping, social capital, resilience and social support are relevant to young mentoring.
- To date, there is no one book that combines youth mentoring and children in care although the potential for how mentoring can benefit children in care is evident.

Note

1 Throughout this report we use the terms: 'children and young people in care', 'children and young people with care experience' and 'care leavers'.

References

Ahrens, K. R., DuBois, D. L., Garrison, M., Spencer, R., Richardson, L. P., & Lozano, P. (2011). Qualitative exploration of relationships with important non-parental adults in the lives of youth in foster care. *Children and Youth Services Review, 33*(6), 1012–1023.

Ahrens, K. R., DuBois, D. L., Richardson, L. P., Fan, M. Y., & Lozano, P. (2008). Youth in foster care with adult mentors during adolescence have improved adult outcomes. *Pediatrics, 121*(2), 246–252.

Avery, R. J., & Freundlich, M. (2009). You're all grown up now: Termination of foster care support at age 18. *Journal of Adolescence, 32*, 247–257.

Baker, C. (2017). *Care leavers views on their transition to adulthood: A rapid review of the evidence.* London: Coram Voice.

Baker, C., Briheim-Crookall, L., Magnus, L., & Selwyn, J. (2019). *Our lives beyond care: Care leavers views on their well-being in 2018.* London: Coram Voice.

Bal, S., Crombez, G., Van Oost, P., & Debourdeaudhuij, I. (2003). The role of social support in well-being and coping with self-reported stressful events in adolescents. *Child Abuse & Neglect, 27*(12), 1377–1395.

Barry, M. M., Clarke, A. M., Morreale, S. E., & Field, C. A. (2018). A review of the evidence on the effects of community-based programs on young people's social and emotional skills development. *Adolescent Research Review*, *3*(1), 13–27.

Bolger, N., & Amarel, D. (2007). Effects of social support visibility on adjustment to stress: Experimental evidence. *Journal of Personality and Social Psychology*, *92*(3), 458–475.

Bowlby, J. (1953). Some pathological processes set in train by early mother-child separation. *Journal of Mental Science*, *99*(415), 265–272.

Brady, B., & Dolan, P. (2007). Exploring good practice in Irish child and family services: Reflections and considerations. *Practice*, *19*(1), 5–18.

Buehler, K. (2017). Relational cultural theory and mentoring in a science support program. *College of science and health theses and dissertations*. 210. Retrieved from http://via.library.depaul.edu/csh_etd/210

Carr, N., & Mayock, P. (2019). *Care and justice: Children and young people in care and contact with the criminal justice system*. Dublin: Irish Penal Reform Trust.

Cassel, J. (1976). The contribution of the social environment to host resistance. *American Journal of Epidemiology*, *104*, 107–123.

Cavell, T. A., & Elledge, L. C. (2014). Mentoring and prevention science. In D. L. DuBois & M. J. Karcher (Eds.), *Handbook of youth mentoring* (pp. 29–43). Thousand Oaks, CA: Sage Publications.

Clarke, A. M., & Clarke, A. D. B. (2003). *Human resilience: A fifty year quest*. London: Kingsley Publishers.

Clayden, J., & Stein, M. (2005). *Mentoring young people leaving care: 'Someone for me'*. York: Joseph Rowntree Foundation.

Cohen, S., & Wills, T. A. (1985). Stress, social support, and the buffering hypothesis. *Psychological Bulletin*, *98*(2), 310.

Coleman, J., & Hendry, L. (1999). *The nature of adolescence* (3rd ed., Adolescence and Society). London and New York, NY: Routledge.

Colley, H. (2003). *Mentoring for social inclusion*. London: Routledge Falmer.

Cooley, C. H. (1902). *Human nature and the social order*. New York, NY: Charles Scribner's Sons.

Côté, J. E. (2014). Towards a new political economy of youth. *Journal of Youth Studies*, *17*(4), 527–543.

Cotterell, J. (2007). *Social networks in youth and adolescence* (2nd ed.). London: Routledge.

Cutrona, C. E. (2000). Social support principles for strengthening families: Messages from America. In J. Canavan, P. Dolan, & J. Pinkerton (Eds.), *Family support: Direction from diversity* (pp. 103–122). London: Jessica Kingsley Publishers.

De Wit, D. J., DuBois, D., Erdem, G., Larose, S., & Lipman, E. L. (2016). The role of program-supported mentoring relationships in promoting youth mental health, behavioral and developmental outcomes, *Prevention Science*, *17*(5), 646–657.

Devaney, C., & McGregor, C. (forthcoming). Protection support and supportive protection for families in the middle: Learning from the Irish context. *Child and Family Social Work*.

Dolan, P., & Brady, B. (2012). *A guide to youth mentoring: Providing effective social support*. London and Philadelphia, PA: Jessica Kingsley Publishers.

Dolan, P., Brady, B., O'Regan, C., Russell, D., Canavan, J., & Forkan, C. (2011). *Big Brothers Big Sisters of Ireland: Evaluation study. Report one: Randomised control trial and implementation report*. Foroige. Retrieved from www.foroige.ie/sites/default/files/big_brother_big_sister_report_3.pdf

DuBois, D. L., Holloway, B. E., Valentine, J. C., & Cooper, H. (2002). Effectiveness of mentoring programs for youth: A meta-analytic review, *American Journal of Community Psychology, 30*(2), 157–197.

Duke, T., Farruggia, S. P., & Germo, G. R. (2017). "I don't know where I would be right now if it wasn't for them": Emancipated foster care youth and their important non-parental adults. *Children and Youth Services Review, 76*, 65–73.

Eccles, J. S., & Gootman, J. A. (2002). Features of positive developmental settings. *Community Programs to Promote Youth Development,* 86–118.

Erickson, E. H. (1968). *Identity: Youth and crisis.* London: Faber & Faber.

Fahlberg, V. (2012). *A child's journey through placement.* London: Jessica Kingsley Publishers.

Farrugia, D. (2013). Young people and structural inequality: Beyond the middle ground. *Journal of Youth Studies, 16*(5), 679–693.

Feldman, S. S., & Elliot, G. R. (1990). *At the threshold: The developing adolescent.* Cambridge, MA: Harvard University Press.

Fletcher, J. K., & Ragins, B. R. (2007). Stone center relational cultural theory: A window on relational mentoring. In B. R. Ragins & K. E. Kram (Eds.), *The handbook of mentoring at work: Theory, research, and practice* (pp. 373–399). Thousand Oaks, CA: Sage Publications.

Freud, S. (1914). On Narcissism: An introduction. In J. Strachey et al. (Trans.), *The standard edition of the complete psychological works of Sigmund Freud*, Volume XIV. London: Hogarth Press.

Frydenberg, E. (2019). *Adolescent coping: Promoting resilience and well-being.* London: Routledge.

Furlong, A. (2013). *Youth studies: An introduction.* Oxford: Routledge.

Garmezy, N. (1993). Risk and resilience. In D. C. Funder, R. D. Parke, C. Tomlinson-Keasey, & K. Widaman (Eds.), *Studying lives through time: Personality and development* (pp. 377–398). Washington, DC: American Psychological Association.

Greeson, J. K., Garcia, A. R., Kim, M., Thompson, A. E., & Courtney, M. E. (2015). Development & maintenance of social support among aged out foster youth who received independent living services: Results from the multi-site evaluation of foster youth programs. *Children and Youth Services Review, 53*, 1–9.

Grotberg, E. H. (1995). *A guide to promoting resilience in children: Strengthening the human spirit.* The Hague, Netherlands: Bernard Van Leer Foundation.

Gypen, L., Vanderfaeillie, J., De Maeyer, S., Belenger, L., & Van Holen, F. (2017). Outcomes of children who grew up in foster care: Systematic-review. *Children and Youth Services Review, 76*, 74–83.

Healey, C. V., & Fisher, P. A. (2011). Young children in foster care and the development of favourable outcomes. *Children and Youth Services Review, 33*(10), 1822–1830.

Herrera, C., Grossman, J. B., Kauh, T. J., Feldman, A. F., & McMaken, J. (2007). *Making a difference in schools: The Big Brothers Big Sisters school-based mentoring impact study.* Philadelphia, PA: Public/Private Ventures.

Hingley-Jones, H., & Ruch, G. (2016). 'Stumbling through'? Relationship-based social work practice in austere times. *Journal of Social Work Practice, 30*(3), 235–248.

Horn, J. P., & Spencer, R. (2018). Natural mentoring to support the establishment of permanency for youth in foster care. In E. Trejos-Castillo & N. Trevino-Schafer (Eds.), *Handbook of foster youth.* New York, NY: Routledge.

Johnson, S. B., Pryce, J. M., & Martinovich, Z. (2011). The role of therapeutic mentoring in enhancing outcomes for youth in foster care. *Child Welfare*, *90*(5), 50–69.

Jordan, J. V. (2013). Relational resilience in girls. In S. Goldstein & R. Brooks (Eds.), *Handbook of resilience in children*. Boston, MA: Springer.

Kersley, H., & Estep, B. (2014). *Relationships for children in care: The value of mentoring and befriending*. London: New Economics Foundation.

Krauss, S. M. (2019, March 12). *These connections are currency some young people need our help to form them*. Retrieved from www.evidencebasedmentoring.org/these-connections-are-currency-some-young-people-need-our-help-to-form-them/

Kupersmidt, J. B., Stump, K. N., Stelter, R. L., & Rhodes, J. E. (2017). Predictors of premature match closure in youth mentoring relationships. *American Journal of Community Psychology*, *59*(1–2), 25–35.

Liebenberg, L., & Ungar, M. (Eds.). (2009). *Researching resilience*. Toronto, ON: University of Toronto Press.

MacLeoid, D., & MacWilliam, M. (1989). *Fionn MacCumhaill* (Seoid nan Gaidheal). Steornabhagh (Stornoway): Acair.

Masten, A. S. (2004). Regulatory processes, risk, and resilience in adolescent development. *Annals of the New York Academy of Sciences*, *1021*(1), 310–319.

Matz, A. K. (2013). Commentary: Do youth mentoring programs work? A review of the empirical literature. *Journal of Juvenile Justice*, *3*(2), 83–101.

McGregor, C., Lynch, M., & Brady, B. (2017). Youth mentoring as a form of support for children and young people at risk: Insights from research and practice. In *The Routledge handbook of global child welfare* (pp. 345–357). Oxon: Routledge.

McMahon, C., & Curtin, C. (2013). The social networks of young people in Ireland with experience of long-term foster care: Some lessons for policy and practice. *Child & Family Social Work*, *18*(3), 329–340.

McKenzie, V., & Frydenberg, E. (2004). Young people and their resources. In E. Frydenberg (Ed), *Thriving, surviving or going under: Coping with everyday lives* (pp. 79–108). Greenwich: Information Age Pub.

Mead, G. H. (1934). *Mind, self and society* (Vol. 111). Chicago: University of Chicago Press.

Miller, J. B. (2008). VI. Connections, disconnections, and violations. *Feminism & Psychology*, *18*(3), 368–380.

Munson, M. R., & McMillen, J. C. (2009). Natural mentoring and psychosocial outcomes among older youth transitioning from foster care. *Children and Youth Services Review*, *31*(1), 104–111.

Munson, M. R., Smalling, S. E., Spencer, R., Scott, L. D. Jr., & Tracy, E. M. (2010). A steady presence in the midst of change: Non-kin natural mentors in the lives of older youth exiting foster care. *Children and Youth Services Review*, *32*(4), 527–535.

Online Etymology Dictionary. (2018). *Mentor*. Retrieved from www.etymonline.com/word/mentor#etymonline_v_12597

Parton, N. (2014a). Social work, child protection and politics: Some critical and constructive reflections. *British Journal of Social Work*, *44*(7), 2042–2056.

Parton, N. (2014b). *The politics of child protection: Contemporary developments and future directions*. London: Macmillan International Higher Education.

Philip, K., & Spratt, J. (2007). *A synthesis of published research on mentoring and befriending*. Manchester: The Mentoring and Befriending Foundation.

Pilisuk, M., & Parks, S. H. (1981). The place of network analysis in the study of supportive social associations. *Basic and Applied Social Psychology, 2*(2), 121–135.

Preston, J. M., Prieto-Flores, Ò., & Rhodes, J. E. (2018). Mentoring in context: A comparative study of youth mentoring programs in the United States and continental Europe. *Youth & Society*. Retrieved from https://doi.org/10.1177/0044118X18813700

Prieto-Flores, Ò., Feu, J., & Casademont, X. (2016). Assessing intercultural competence as a result of internationalization at home efforts: A case study from the nightingale mentoring program. *Journal of Studies in International Education, 20*(5), 437–453.

Putnam, R. D. (2000). Bowling alone: America's declining social capital. In *Culture and politics* (pp. 223–234). New York, NY: Palgrave Macmillan.

Ragins, B. R. (2012). Relational mentoring: A positive approach to mentoring at work. *The Oxford handbook of positive organizational scholarship* (pp. 519–536). Oxford: Oxford University Press.

Raposa, E. B., Ben-Eliyahu, A., Olsho, L. E., & Rhodes, J. (2019). Birds of a feather: Is matching based on shared interests and characteristics associated with longer youth mentoring relationships? *Journal of Community Psychology, 47*(2), 385–397.

Rhodes, J. E. (2005). A model of youth mentoring. In D. L. DuBois & M. J. Karcher (Eds.), *Handbook of youth mentoring* (pp. 30–43). Thousand Oaks, CA: Sage Publications.

Rhodes, J. E., Grossman, J. B., & Resch, N. L. (2000). Agents of change: Pathways through which mentoring relationships influence adolescents' academic adjustment. *Child Development, 71*(6), 1662–1671.

Rhodes, J. E., Haight, W. L., & Briggs, E. C. (1999). The influence of mentoring on the peer relationships of foster youth in relative and nonrelative care. *Journal of Research on Adolescence, 9*(2), 185–201.

Rhodes, J. E., Spencer, R., Keller, T. E., Liang, B., & Noam, G. (2006). A model for the influence of mentoring relationships on youth development. *Journal of Community Psychology, 34*(6), 691–707.

Rutter, M. (2012). Resilience: Causal pathways and social ecology. In M. Ungar (Ed.), *The social ecology of resilience: A handbook of theory and practice* (pp. 33–42). New York, NY: Springer.

Samuels, G. M., & Pryce, J. M. (2008). "What doesn't kill you makes you stronger": Survivalist self-reliance as resilience and risk among young adults aging out of foster care. *Children and Youth Services Review, 30*(10), 1198–1210.

Santrock, J. W. (2012). *Adolescence*. New York, NY: McGrow-Hill Companies.

Schwartz, S. E., Lowe, S. R., & Rhodes, J. E. (2012). Mentoring relationships and adolescent self-esteem. *The Prevention Researcher, 19*(2), 17.

Seden, J. (2002). Underpinning theories for the assessment of children's needs. In H. Ward & W. Rose (Eds.), *Approaches to needs assessment in children's service* (pp. 195–216). London and New York, NY: Jessica Kingsley Publishers.

Selwyn, J., & Riley, S. (2015). *Children and young people's views on being in care: A literature review*. Bristol: University of Bristol & Coram Voice.

Shildrick, T., & MacDonald, R. (2006). *Understanding youth exclusion: Critical moments, social networks and social capital* (ESRC Seminar Series on Mentoring and Social Policy), Manchester Metropolitan University, Manchester, UK.

Simões, F., & Alarcão, M. (2014). Promoting well-being in school-based mentoring through the satisfaction of basic psychological needs: Does it really count? *Journal of Happiness Studies*, 15(2), 407–424.

Singer, E. R., Berzin, S. C., & Hokanson, K. (2013). Voices of former foster youth: Supportive relationships in the transition to adulthood. *Children and Youth Services Review*, 35(12), 2110–2117.

Smokowski, P. R., & Holland Kopasz, K. (2005). Bullying in school: An overview of types, effects, family characteristics, and intervention strategies. *Children & Schools*, 27(2), 101–110.

Southwick, S. M., Morgan III, C. A., Vythilingam, M., & Charney, D. (2007). Mentors enhance resilience in at-risk children and adolescents. *Psychoanalytic Inquiry*, 26(4), 577–584.

Spencer, R. (2012). A working model of mentors' contributions to youth mentoring relationship quality: Insights from research on psychotherapy. *LEARNing Landscapes*, 5(2), 295–312.

Spencer, R., Gowdy, G., Drew, A. L., & Rhodes, J. E. (2019). "Who Knows Me the Best and Can Encourage Me the Most?": Matching and early relationship development in youth-initiated mentoring relationships with system-involved youth. *Journal of Adolescent Research*, 34(1), 3–29.

Spencer, R., Tugenberg, T., Ocean, M., Schwartz, S. E., & Rhodes, J. E. (2016). "Somebody Who Was on My Side" a qualitative examination of youth initiated mentoring. *Youth & Society*, 48(3), 402–424.

Stanton-Salazar, R. D. (2011). A social capital framework for the study of institutional agents and their role in the empowerment of low-status students and youth. *Youth & Society*, 43(3), 1066–1109.

Stein, M. (2012). *Young people leaving care, supporting pathways to adulthood*. London: Jessica Kingsley Publishers.

Stein, M., & Munro, E. M. (2008). *Transitions from care to adulthood: International research and practice*. London: Jessica kingsley Publishers.

Sutton, L., & Stack, N. (2012). Hearing quiet voices: Biological children's experiences of fostering. *British Journal of Social Work*, 43(3), 596–612.

Thompson, A. E., Greeson, J. K., & Brunsink, A. M. (2016). Natural mentoring among older youth in and aging out of foster care: A systematic review. *Children and Youth Services Review*, 61, 40–50.

Tolan, P. H., Henry, D. B., Schoeny, M. S., Lovegrove, P., & Nichols, E. (2014). Mentoring programs to affect delinquency and associated outcomes of youth at risk: A comprehensive meta-analytic review. *Journal of Experimental Criminology*, 10(2), 179–206.

Van Dam, L., Smit, D., Wildschut, B., Branje, S. J. T., Rhodes, J. E., Assink, M., & Stams, G. J. J. M. (2018). Does natural mentoring matter? A multilevel meta-analysis on the association between natural mentoring and youth outcomes. *American Journal of Community Psychology*, 62(1–2), 203–220.

Winter, K., Cree, V., Hallett, S., Hadfield, M., Ruch, G., Morrison, F., & Holland, S. (2016). Exploring communication between social workers, children and young people. *British Journal of Social Work*, 47(5), 1427–1444.

2 Children in care and leaving care
Issues and challenges

2.1 Introduction

While, at its core, the care system is guided by a philosophy of protection and support for the young person, the potential negative impacts of care experiences are well established. As a result of their experience prior to entering care and whilst in care, young people can experience a range of different challenges caused by intrinsic (e.g. behavioural and mental health related issues) and extrinsic difficulties (e.g. environmental and family related). Even for the most resilient and well supported, the experience of being in formal care for many children brings with it a range of challenges posed by usually having to manage the dual identity with foster or residential home and family of origin relations and context. It also usually involves having various formal social and possible legal professionals involved in one's life and often means limited opportunities for building their own natural informal support system for their futures. A lot of research evidence shows that the formal social work and support systems children in care and their families have are effective in many ways but do not always meet expectations or need. Over-reliance on specialist services and lack of continuity of care are also factors that have been highlighted. When the time for leaving care comes at age 18, research indicates that transitioning to adulthood can be a very different process for youth in care, compared to members of their peer group who were not in care.

This chapter draws from relevant literature and research to provide a commentary on the range of socio-emotional needs of children in care and leaving care. It is based on the knowledge of the importance of informal social support for service users alongside dedicated formal social support for persons in need (Devaney, Gillen, Landy, & Canavan, 2013; Devaney, 2011; McMahon & Curtin, 2013). This must include support to young people in care, foster carers, foster carers' children and families of origin and be framed from a systemic ecological perspective. The discussion in this chapter aims to highlight the potential role that a mentor can fulfil. The chapter begins with a brief overview of definitions of care and what this means. It then considers the socio-emotional needs of children in care and leaving care based on existing literature.

2.2 Brief overview of definitions of 'care'

Petrowski, Cappa, and Gross (2017) have attempted to estimate the number of children in care internationally. While showing the challenges of such a calculation, especially for those in foster care given the many versions of alternative family care that exist, it is believed that approximately 2.5 million are in residential care alone. Across the globe, there are variations in use of language to denote 'care', differing constructions of care and thus the types of state support provided in such circumstances (Courtney & Thoburn, 2009).

Formal alternative care refers to public-welfare supported arrangements, or private arrangements coming under statutory governance arrangements, from children living out of their own homes. It is defined by the United Nations as 'all care provided in a family environment which has been ordered by a competent administrative body or judicial authority, and all care provided in a residential environment' (UN Guidelines for Alternative Care, 2010, p. 6). Formal alternative care includes the following arrangements:

- 'Foster care' meaning a placement with parents who have been selected and trained to look after children on a short or a long term basis
- 'Kinship care' as a subset of 'foster care' where a relative is selected and trained specifically to look after a child on a short or long term basis
- 'Other forms of family based care' are also noted in the UN guidelines though not specified
- 'Residential care' refers to arrangements where children are looked after in group settings rather than family based settings
- 'Group care' is a subset of residential care meaning a placement organised around a small group home model employing child care workers/professionals to support a small number of children within a unit
- 'Secure/special care' as a subset of group care which is organised for individuals or small groups to provide intensive professional support and protection for a young person with complex needs and/or behaviour
- 'Institutional care' can be seen as another subset of residential care meaning a larger unit with perhaps multiple group homes or one large unit to house multiple numbers of children
- 'Individual supervised care' is another form of care identified by the UN Guidelines on Alternative care (2010, p. 6) as 'Supervised independent living arrangements for children'
- 'Adoption for care' is an outcome that can happen through legislation in many jurisdictions whereby children who are in long-term care can be legally adopted by existing or newly recruited adoptive parents. In these instances, adoption is normally open maintaining some contact, where appropriate and possible, with families of origin

The UN Guidelines on Alternative care recognise the different forms of formal care but place family based care as the ideal arrangement for younger children, especially children under the age of three. Where residential care is used, the recommendations are that a policy of deinstitutionalisation is established by the state and that standards for care are in place. The UN guidelines also set down the expectations from states to protect and support children in care and those who are looking after them.

In addition to formal care – family and institution based – it is important to also recognise the significance and scope of informal care outside of formally supported kinship care. The UN Guidelines define this as 'any private arrangement provided in a family environment, whereby the child is looked after on an ongoing or indefinite basis by relatives or friends (informal kinship care) or by others in their individual capacity, at the initiative of the child, his/her parents or other person without this arrangement having been ordered by an administrative or judicial authority or a duly accredited body' (2010, p. 6). This can relate to arrangements under legislation on guardianship. Orphans cared for by surviving family are another category to note as well as other arrangements made outside of court processes. Nandy and Selwyn (2012) carried out a large scale study of kinship fostering in the United Kingdom finding that many of those in informal kinship arrangements were living in poor and deprived circumstances. A similar issue is evident in many other international contexts where kinship carers outside of the 'care system' are supported through social welfare only and not in receipt of any special formal support services. How these arrangements can be better supported through formal care support systems is a matter for ongoing research and concern and the value of mentoring in such instances is potentially equally valid.

Finally in relation to definitions of care, the care period is important to briefly mention. Children can come into care for short periods or for their whole childhood. Definitions of long term care vary by country and region but usually relate to children being in care where the plan is that, for at least the foreseeable future if not until age 18, they will be in alternative care. The needs for support for children and young people in care will vary depending on their expected timescale.

2.3 The importance of understanding diversity of care experience

Whatever the form of care we speak about, it is important to note that it is not always a clear-cut demarcation between being in care and being at home. Sometimes dual care arrangements may be in place as well as different informal, supported or unsupported, arrangements in different contexts. A common feature across these domains is that children require alternative care because their parent(s) of origin or guardians are not able to look after them, have died or have been found to be abusive or neglectful to them. With regard to capacity to care, the reasons for this may be intrinsic to the carer linked to substance abuse/addiction, disability or mental health problems for example. They may also be extrinsic to the person and due to socio-economic or socio-social conditions that make it impossible for them to care for their child. Even though the UN Guidelines on alternative care state that 'financial and material poverty, or conditions directly and uniquely imputable to such poverty, should never be the only justification for the removal of a child from parental care' (UN Guidelines for Alternative Care, 2010, p. 4), unfortunately poverty and lack of support to families plays a major role in influencing and majorly adding to the care population globally (Bywaters et al., 2016; McGhee et al., 2017).

Increasingly, there is a shift in focus towards early intervention, prevention, use of adoption from care and use of kinship care as demonstrated in a UK comparative study although more systematic comparisons of data across countries is needed to develop this analysis (McGhee et al., 2017). Globally, there is a strong movement towards deinstitutionalisation and a growing body of research and practice has developed to progress this field (Mulheir & Berridge, 2017).However, the extensive ongoing use of residential care in some contexts must also be recognised (Thoburn & Ainsworth, 2015) and the range of different therapeutic models applied understood (Thompson, Duppong Hurley, Trout, Huefner, & Daly, 2017; Whittaker, 2017). The need for sustained consideration of the use of residential care is also demonstrated in the work of López and del Valle (2013) in relation to the high proportion of children in residential care in Spain. This seems to be the result of a range of factors including age of entry to care (older children), prevalence of significant behavioural and mental health needs and lack of alternatives in family care options. Their article highlights the importance of not over-simplifying the problematization of group care. They also indicate the urgency of a global effort to address the achievement of suitable care placements for children who require it and to make a call for increasing efforts in relation to prevention and family support to try, into the future, to reduce the number of children whose circumstances become such that they need to be in care in the first instance. Steels and Simpson (2017) also support the position that while foster care is usually favoured especially in traditional Western context, the importance of quality and support of appropriate residential care settings is also important. Generally, while the global movement is broadly to shift away from residential to family based care (Mulheir & Gyllensten, 2017), the needs for support of children in such institutions should not be ignored until such time as this occurs and ways to reduce potential harmful effects of group care continually developed (Groza & McCreery-Bunkers, 2017; Mollidor & Berridge, 2017).

Another common feature for children in alternative care is that it is rare that the child's circumstances is in any way a result of their own making and far more likely that it is a situation imposed upon them. For some children, coming into care can be a sanctuary from abuse and harm at home while for others, it is a heartbreaking removal from family ties often not just from parents but from grandparents, siblings, extended family and local community and friends. For many, it brings with it a range of emotions around separation, loss, attachment, trauma, bereavement (Healey & Fisher, 2011). Different needs also arise for young people with a disability coming into care (McConkey, Kelly, & Craig, 2012). It is important therefore to emphasise from the outset that we should not attempt to generalise the care experience. We need to appreciate the diversity as expressed by young people in care and their carers who get the opportunity to share their stories and educate us about this diversity.

2.4 Life course trajectories of children in care

While services and responses in relation to children in care are usually organised in terms of support children receive pre-care, in care and transitioning from care/after care, it is important not to separate these out conceptually. The care experience of a child, for a short or long term period, is part of their life course and trajectory that can often have a strong bearing on their identity, experiences, relationships and social context throughout their lives. A life course view is essential as the care experience, long or short term, will form part of the child's adult identity and memories (Brady & Gilligan, 2018). The way in which young people are facilitated to map out their life course and networks around them can have a major impact on their emotional and psychological well-being. Increasingly with regard to young people transitioning out of care, the importance of a life course perspective that looks to long as well as immediate and short term care transition is essential. The particular importance of a life course approach to supporting young people in care with their education specifically is demonstrated in recent work by Brady and Gilligan (2018) who argue that such a life course perspective is necessary to inform research and produce a deeper understanding of educational progress for children and young people in care.

The importance of a life course approach transcends any particular type of welfare or care regime and has universal resonance for those involved in supporting the life transition for children and young people. For example, Cameron, Reimer, and Smith (2016) consider foster care in 11 European countries and discuss the importance of foster care as fulfilling an upbringing role on behalf of society that embeds the passing on of cultural heritage and the consolidation of cross-generational relations. Mertz and Andersen (2017), using a population study in Denmark, highlight also the importance of a life course viewpoint to take into account the intergenerational transmission of disadvantage that can lead to care experiences and the higher likelihood of care-experienced children to have children in care. It is a complex issue without easy solution but it highlights the lifelong impact care can have not just on emotional but also access to practical resources that can increase the risk of disadvantage. Focusing specifically on kinship care, Connolly, Kiraly, McCrae, and Mitchell (2017, p. 93) argue for the importance of a life course approach that takes account of inter-generational relations and four life course domains that are: 'child-centred; relationship-supportive; family and culturally responsive; and system focused'.

2.5 Coping and resilience

It is well established that young people often need help coping with being in care (Fernandez, 2009; Farmer, Selwyn, & Meakings, 2013). One of the remarkable points to note early on is the evidence of the ability to cope and the resilience of children and young people during their lives in care and afterwards (Stein, 2012). Theories relating to the sociology of childhood and the social ecology of resilience emphasise the relationships between individual agency and wider social context in influencing resilience for young people in care (Berridge, 2017) (with specific reference to resilience and educational outcomes). Referring specifically to residential care, Schofield, Larsson, and Ward (2017) found that all main factors that affected whether young people made successful transitions to early adult life are linked to resilience. These factors were: connection, agency, activity and coherence.

An approach that recognises potential and resilience comes from strengths rather than a problem-focused approach. This should not however detract from the reality of certain challenges experienced and the need sometimes for intensive and specialist help and support to cope. Any strategies aimed at supporting ability to cope for the persons in care or their carers needs also to be balanced with recognition that some situations – such as limited resources, structural inequalities or unfair and unequal distribution of services – need to be addressed through advocacy and challenging if necessary rather than helping to cope in unreasonable circumstances.

2.6 Dealing with stigma of being in care

Being in care brings with it, in many contexts, an inherent stigma that links strongly with the history of care in many countries. For example, in Ireland the Commission to Inquire into Child Abuse (2009) reported with great detail a litany of abuse of children in residential care in Ireland during the 20th century. There were many reasons for this systematic abuse to have been allowed to occur and is reflective of disclosures in other countries also (Wright, Swain, & McPhillips, 2017). One of these factors was an inherent prejudice against the children residing in so-called industrial schools in Ireland due to their status as being from extreme poverty or illegitimate (Buckley & McGregor, 2018).

In present times, studies from young people in care and having left care continue to highlight the fact that being in care is seen in many ways as a stigma that affects social attitudes and a young person's own social perception (see e.g. Dima & Skehill, 2011; Selwyn & Riley, 2015). Because the reasons for children being in care can include experiences of abuse and neglect, it can be embarrassing and upsetting for children and young people to talk openly about this experience. Sometimes parents' actions (e.g. wilful neglect/deliberate harm/persistent substance abuse) bring social judgement that impacts on the children. As Rogers (2016) found, children and young people develop strategies to deal with this stigma and advises that services need to value the importance of friendship groups to counteract stigma and develop more opportunities to bring fostered young people together. Other strategies can include creating public awareness and understanding about care and reasons for children being in different forms of care. Organisations that collectively support young people in care, such as EPIC in Ireland, are crucial to enable young people to come together to share their experiences and challenge public views and opinion. Public and community responsibility to address issues of stigma and subsequent prejudice, discrimination and oppression must also be emphasised.

2.7 Impact of pre-care experiences

No matter how a child or young person is doing in care and afterwards, they are there because of something having happened in their life with their parent/family they were born into or residing full time with and/or the community they were from. Even if removed and placed at birth, the child still has a family experience and identity preceding this experience. The importance of attention to the pre-care experience is highlighted in studies such as Gilligan (2000), Farmer et al. (2013), Vanderfaille, Van Holen, Vanschoonlandt, Robberechts, and Stroobants (2013). Keeping with the argument about a life course approach above, the pre-care experience of young people is essential to recognise and appreciate not just at the moment of placement but as a continuity throughout and beyond the person's experience in care. Life story work (See Fahlberg, 2012) is a common practice used by many working with children in care in the United Kingdom and Ireland and many excellent examples of how to use this work to help a person in care connect their past and present are available internationally. This kind of work should be an ongoing process, tailored for different developmental stages for the child/young person (e.g. during adolescence and how issues of identity arise) and the needs and interests of the individual person (Fahlberg, 2012). It should also be carried out within a broad ecological framework that recognises the significant interactions between a child's micro and meso systems and internal issues alongside the wider exo and macro levels (see Devaney et al). The chrono level is especially important in relation to life story work as it helps to emphasise that different moments in time, during the course of the child's life before, during and after, will bring different challenges and issues to address through life story work.

When supporting young people in care through life story work and other forms of support, the potential impact of pre-care experience is crucially important to be aware of. This may be especially the case for children and young people placed in care later in their lives. A balance needs to be struck between respecting the privacy and intimacy of the person's past experience and creating an environment and relationship of trust to allow for appropriate communication and dialogue. Awareness of barriers to talking about the past is important. For the young person, this could be a fear of upsetting the foster carer, feeling torn between the family of origin and foster family and fear of loved ones being judged. For those supporting the young people, issues about confidentiality, appropriate disclosure and care not to open up histories that cause re-traumatisation are the key. Clarity of role and purpose and professional support is the key.

2.8 Evidence of indicators of poorer outcomes for children in care regarding education, mental health, well-being and behavioural issues

Children in care are likely to be more at risk of experiencing relatively less positive outcomes for health, education and well-being (Stein, 2012; Stein & Munro, 2008; Gypen, Vanderfaeillie, De Maeyer, Belenger, & Van Holen, 2017). While multiple factors can counteract this, such as family stability, resilience, personal motivation, good social support, it is important to be cognisant of the particular challenge experienced by children in care of achieving good outcomes for their future especially with regard to mental health, education and well-being. Gypen et al. (2017, p. 74) for example in a review of studies of 32 outcomes for children in foster care conclude that:

> The results are clear as well as troubling. In both systems, children who leave care continue to struggle on all areas (education, employment, income, housing, health, substance abuse and criminal involvement) compared to their peers from the general population. A stable foster care placement, establishing a foothold in education and having a steady figure (mentor) who supports youth after they age out of care seem to be important factors to improve the outcomes.

It is of interest to note that in 1972, Napier wrote an article about predictive outcomes for children in care including a detailed examination of factors such as the child's behaviour, relation with parents, foster parent context and so on and concluded that: 'Examination of the different tables shows that, in almost every case, regardless of the child's circumstances there was at least a 50% chance of success' (p. 332), showing how difficult it is to predict outcomes based in circumstances. They recognise the 'advantages in knowing which children may need most support, and at what stage of placement they are at risk' while at the same time warn caution of assuming others may not succeed: 'Children will continue to surprise us in their ability to make the most unexpected relationships, and in their refusal to conform to our preconceived ideas. There are many occasions in social work when it is good for our doubts to be proved wrong – the successful outcome of a difficult placement is such an occasion' (p. 332).

Even though we have come a long way since then in terms of evidenced outcomes, the fact remains that while we can attempt to predict different outcomes depending on characteristics intrinsic and extrinsic to the child, it remains the case that (1) we must accept that usually a child is in care because of a form of adversity in the first instance and (2) that irrespective of that, strong relationships, excellent support, communication and continuity do improve the chances of better outcomes than disruption, poor connections, multiple transitions and limited attachments. This emphasises the importance of interventions with young people in care that attends not only to their practical and developmental outcomes but also their social and emotional well-being outcomes. In addition, financial and material resources are important. For example, Andersen (2012) in a large study of almost 16,000 children in Denmark found that while there was great variation in the factors that affected outcomes, children in families with better resources were found to experience less complex placement journeys than those with fewer resources. Mendis, Lehmann, and Gardner (2017) attribute many of the negative outcomes such as poverty, homelessness, addiction and mental health problems to lack of educational or vocational qualifications. They consider how a focus on promoting academic success can result in better outcomes and conclude that two main factors are key; a conducive environment including 'valuing of education, social networks, practical and financial resources' and 'personal factors' including 'resilience and motivating factors' (p. 106). Brown and Bailey-Etta (2018) explore the specific issues relating to out of home care in the United States and the overrepresentation of African American children, linking this to the impact of poverty and social problems and the inadequacy of the out of home care system in being able to address this.

2.9 The challenge of managing dual identity and dual systems within an ecological context

As aforementioned, it is important to situate children in care within their wider ecological context (Bronfenbrenner, 1979; Bronfenbrenner & Morris, 2007). With this frame in mind, one of the most challenging things about being in care can be the fact that for most children, it means taking on a dual or multiple identity and operating within at least two ecological systems, as argued by Moran, McGregor, and Devaney (2017). For those in instable placements or experiencing moves between residential or foster placements, they will experience an even more complex set of interactions within their ecological system. Young people need a great deal of support managing this duality and complexity, taking onboard an ecological perspective that can map the relevant interactions and relationships at micro, meso, exo, macro and chrono level for the individual in care. When relationships and placements are disrupted, this is even more challenging. Skoog, Khoo, and Nygren (2012) for example highlight the impact of lack of continuity of relationship with social worker and disrupted care placement on children in Sweden showing the in-depth emotional impact it has on young people while at same time their resilience and ability to adapt to new environments. Contact and access with parents/family of origin brings this matter particularly to the fore (Biehal, 2012; Kiraly & Humphreys, 2016). The literature highlights the challenge of balancing the principle that contact and access with family is essential for maintaining ties, identity and relationships; although it can also be fraught with challenges (Boyle, 2017)

The need to take an ecological perspective, rather than just a linear one, between parent and child, is essential to take onboard the importance of the wider family of siblings, grandparents, aunts, uncles and so on in relation to maintaining access and contact. Research shows often the maintenance of relationships outside of the parental guardianship connections are neglected; thus the young person in care, especially long term care, loses access to important relationships and informal supports.

2.10 Becoming independent and transitioning from care – additional challenges

While we have argued that care experience should be viewed from a life course and life trajectory viewpoint, it is important also to consider the particular needs and issues for young people at the point of transition to adulthood. Concern about this aspect of care received research and policy attention in many systems later than attention to needs of children in care. As Winter (2012) argues, research shows the impact of multiple transitions on young people's social and emotional well-being. The UN Alternative Care guidance clearly emphasises the importance of preparation for and support in leaving care. In the past 20 years specifically, a number of researchers have studied the core issues relating to children leaving care. Mike Stein's early research describes different approaches to transitions and the importance of resilience as an underpinning concept (Stein, 2008, 2012). Stein refers to three different groups of young people: the 'moving on group', the survivors group' and the 'victims group'. Outcomes are better generally for young people when they have continuity and support from their foster families for example (see Christiansen, Havnen, Havik, & Andersen, 2012) and, conversely, those without a source of reliable adult support are most in need of additional supports.

John Pinkerton proposes that transitions should be understood with a broad socio-ecological context that moves away from seeing matters in a linear way only between young person and family. His social ecology model for young people leaving care (Pinkerton, 2011) offers a model where a number of potential sources of informal and formal support can be identified. As Coyle and Pinkerton (2012, p. 298) argue with regard to Northern

Ireland, which is an area that has had significant policy and research in this area:

> Transition from state care needs to be understood as a complex process of making connections within and across formal and informal social systems – it is about the social ecology of young peoples' lives. In regard to the formal systems that contribute to that social ecology, four key components deserve attention: law and policy; planning; service delivery; and monitoring, evaluation and research. . . . The needs of specific groups leaving care, who may have additional needs, remains an area for further development as is the development of more longitudinal studies'.

Dinisman and Zeira (2011) likewise take an ecological approach to understanding young people leaving care focusing on three levels of individual, social support and institutional characteristics. Refaeli, Mangold, Zeira, and Köngeter (2017) consider the impact of continuity and discontinuity on the transition experience for young people, highlighting the importance of continuity where possible. Moran et al. (2017) likewise found continuity to be a core theme emerging from their study of factors impacting on stability of children in care and leaving care. The importance of a life course viewpoint is reflected in the work of Sulimani-Aidan (2016) who argues insufficient attention is paid to the future expectations of young people in care and the impact this can have on their resilience.

2.11 The impact of having professional services involved in children and young people's day-to-day lives

Something that stands out for children in care compared to many of their peers is that they must have formal professional services involved in their lives such as residential care staff and/or social care and social work practitioners visiting and supporting them in foster care. The relationship with social workers and social services has a major influence on the experiences of young people in care and their families (McEvoy & Smith, 2011; Moran, McGregor, & Devaney, 2016). Over-reliance on specialist services and lack of continuity of care are factors that have been highlighted in research (McEvoy & Smith, 2011, p. 24). While regular support, monitoring and review of children in care is absolutely essential, it is important to highlight how this may feel for the young persons themselves. Sutton and Stack (2012) and Serbinski and Brown (2016) provide rich insight into the views and experiences of children of foster families in relation to how it was for them to have child welfare workers involved in their home. Connolly, White, and Satka (2017) provide a detailed commentary on the challenges and potential of co-production of services with children and families including foster care families giving insight into the experiences of the children and young people's families which is likely to colour their own views and experiences of partnership and co-production. For example, they highlight how traditionally the power of the statutory state system has been a deterrent to engaging parents and young people in partnership, offering many explanations for this, including a view that parents can be defensive against child protection systems and cautious about levels of trustful engagement and power relations. They also cite various research showing the ingredients that improve relationships and co-production that include partnership, trust, a feeling of being taken seriously and involvement in the assessment and intervention processes. While studies show that children in care are often more positive about their experiences than their parents of origin are, it remains the case that having a social worker or residential care key worker may be a source of embarrassment itself for young people in the context of their peers and a source of exclusion or feeling of difference even when the formal relationship is a positive one.

Another issue to consider is how often children and young people who come into care lose their connection with more informal sources of support and protection. McGregor, Lynch, and Brady (2017) show, for example, how often in situations of high levels of need or risk for children and families, including working with children in care, there is a tendency to under-utilise informal supports like mentoring and focus only on the formal services like social work. Through commentary on the provision of the Big Brother Big Sister mentoring programme in Ireland, they explore the benefits and limits of using mentoring for young people with higher or more complex level of need. The authors argue for the consideration of mentoring not as alternative to formal professional services but as a 'crucially beneficial supplementary service' (McGregor et al., 2017, p. 356).

2.12 Permanence and stability

For all children in alternative care, the ideal is that in the absence of their being able to live in their families/homes of origin, that they have security and a sense of permanence in their alternative home. The theme of stability and permanence is prominent within most research and writing relating to children in care. Two relatively recent literature reviews – Rock, Michelson, Thomson, and Day (2013) and Moran et al. (2016) – provide a comprehensive overview of the field from an international perspective. The studies show the number of intrinsic and extrinsic factors that affect placement stability, and yet only a few are very strong indicators of likely positive or negative outcomes. This is not for the lack of quality of research and analysis and more a reflection of the complexities involved that make it very difficult to generalise. However, age at entry to care is consistently found to have an influence, with early entry more associated with greater likelihood of stability (Khoo, Skoog, & Dalin, 2012; McSherry et al., 2010). The presence of serious mental health or behavioural problems can lead to instability.

Otherwise, many complex factors influence permanence as shown in the synthesis by Roarty, Leinster, McGregor, and Moran (2018), which summarises factors as follows. For internal factors, they identify: mental health; behavioural and emotional development; age at entry to care; confidence and self-identity; realising potential in foster care; school experiences and prior experiences of trauma, abuse and neglect. For external factors, they identify number of placement moves; stability of the family structure; foster carer's ability to cope; foster carer's health and economic resources; the quality of social and services supports; differing expectations between the foster family and the foster child; relationships with families of origin and relationships with social workers (Roarty et al., 2018, pp. 53–54).

2.13 Addressing the future challenges of care: priorities for action

Davidson, Milligan, Quinn, Cantwell, and Elsley (2017) carried out a critical review of the UN Guidelines on Alternative Care referred to above. They summarise how the trend has become globally towards family based care and comment on the range of practices in place towards deinstitutionalisation. The authors identify three main challenges that exist in relation to implementing the alternative care guidance. These are: deinstitutionalisation, adequate resourcing for family based care and the development and support of kinship care. It is also important to recognise that for young people in care, they are facing many of the challenges shared by their peers such as influence of living in a digital age on social and peer relations (Sen, 2015). With regard to social and emotional needs of young people in care, the importance of relationships and a sense of belonging (Biehal, 2012) cannot be over-emphasised along with the need for excellent social support and communication between all aspects of a person's eco-system.

Throughout this chapter, time and time again, the importance of relationships has been referred to. This centrality of supporting relationships and maintaining continuity in the lives of young people in care is emphasised by Vera Fahlberg (2012) amongst many other experts in the field. A critical awareness of the impact of external factors like lack of mental health support, poor educational support or inadequate formal supports from the child welfare agency is essential to maintain.

2.14 Conclusion

In sum, this chapter has provided an overview of the kind of particular issues that need to be attended to when working with and supporting young people in care. The importance of sensitivity and empathy towards the challenges we have summarised above is highlighted. The need for comprehensive supportive services for persons in care and their carers is also evident and the impact of lack of such support severe in many instances.

Our argument in this book is that formal agency supports through social work, specialist mental health, educational and welfare services are essential to support children in care. Youth mentoring can be an excellent additional and enduring resource as discussed in Chapter 4.

> **Summary points:** *children in care and leaving care – issues and challenges*
>
> - Current research shows the range of themes that need to be considered are regularly reviewed, updated and taken account of in care planning and support.
> - There is strong research evidence to show the negative outcomes for children and young people in care because of factors outside of their control and the need for improved attention to the quality of their education, health care, social welfare and wider social supports.
> - Despite many efforts by those supporting children in care, evidence shows us that outcomes for education continue to be poorer on average. This limits the life chances of the young person in care with potentially lifelong negative consequences.
> - The importance of a life course perspective ensures that recognition of experiences prior to care and planning into the future from care is given due regard.
> - An ecological approach is important to highlight the interactions between the internal and external contexts for young people that are dynamic and changing over time and place.
> - A strengths based approach ensures a balance between recognising challenges and identifying and supporting strengths within and around the child or young person.
> - There is a dominant worldwide approach aimed at strengthening family based care through the better resourcing of family based care, wider use of kinship care and deinstitutionalisation.

References

Andersen, S. H. (2012). Complex patterns: On the characteristics of children who experience high and low degrees of foster-care drift. *British Journal of Social Work*, 44(6), 1545–1562.

Berridge, D. (2017). The education of children in care: Agency and resilience. *Children and Youth Services Review*, 77, 86–93.

Biehal, N. (2012). A sense of belonging: Meanings of family and home in long-term foster care. *British Journal of Social Work*, 44(4), 955–971.

Boyle, C. (2017). 'What is the impact of birth family contact on children in adoption and long-term foster care?' A systematic review. *Child & Family Social Work*, 22, 22–33.

Brady, E., & Gilligan, R. (2018). The life course perspective: An integrative research paradigm for examining the educational experiences of adult care leavers? *Children and Youth Services Review*, 87, 69–77.

Bronfenbrenner, U. (1979). *The ecology of human development*. Cambridge: Harvard University Press.

Bronfenbrenner, U., & Morris, P. A. (2007). The bioecological model of human development. In W. Damon & R. M. Lerner (Eds.), *Handbook of child psychology, Vol. 1: Theoretical models of human development* (6th ed., pp. 793–828). Hoboken, NJ: Wiley.

Brown, A. W., & Bailey-Etta, B. (2018). An out-of-home care system in crisis: Implications for African American children in the child welfare system. In S. Brissett-Chapman (Ed.), *Serving African American children* (pp. 65–84). New York, NY: Routledge.

Buckley, S. A., & McGregor, C. (2018). Interrogating institutionalisation and child welfare: The Irish case, 1939–1991. *European Journal of Social Work*, 1–11.

Bywaters, P., Bunting, L., Davidson, G., Hanratty, J., Mason, W., McCartan, C., & Steils, N. (2016). *The relationship between poverty, child abuse and neglect: An evidence review*. New York, NY: Joseph Rowntree Foundation.

Cameron, C., Reimer, D., & Smith, M. (2016). Towards a theory of upbringing in foster care in Europe. *European Journal of Social Work*, 19(2), 152–170.

Christiansen, Ø., Havnen, K. J., Havik, T., & Anderssen, N. (2012). Cautious belonging: Relationships in long-term foster-care. *British Journal of Social Work*, 43(4), 720–738.

Connolly, M., Kiraly, M., McCrae, L., & Mitchell, G. (2017). A kinship care practice framework: Using a life course approach. *The British Journal of Social Work*, 47(1), 87–105.

Connolly, N., White, L., & Satka, M. (2017). From relationship-based practice in child welfare services to co-production with families. In P. Dolan & N. Frost (Eds.), *The Routledge handbook of global child welfare* (pp. 315–325). London and New York, NY: Taylor & Francis.

Courtney, M., & Thoburn, J. (2009). *Children in state care*. London: Routledge.

Coyle, D., & Pinkerton, J. (2012). Leaving care: The need to make connections. *Child Care in Practice*, 18(4), 297–308.

Davidson, J. C., Milligan, I., Quinn, N., Cantwell, N., & Elsley, S. (2017). Developing family-based care: Complexities in implementing the UN guidelines for the alternative care of children. *European Journal of Social Work*, 20(5), 754–769.

Devaney, C. (2011). *Family support as an approach to working with children and families in Ireland: An explorative study of past and present perspectives among pioneers and practitioners* (Doctoral dissertation), School of Political Science and Sociology, NUI Galway.

Devaney, C., Gillen, A., Landy, F., & Canavan, J. (2013). *What works in family support?* Dublin: HSE.

Dima, G., & Skehill, C. (2011). Making sense of leaving care: The contribution of Bridges model of transition to understanding the psycho-social process. *Children and Youth Services Review*, 33(12), 2532–2539.

Dinisman, T., & Zeira, A. (2011). The contribution of individual, social support and institutional characteristics to perceived readiness to leave care in Israel: An ecological perspective. *British Journal of Social Work*, 41(8), 1442–1458.

Fahlberg, V. (2012). *A child's journey through placement*. London: Jessica Kingsley Publishers.

Farmer, E., Selwyn, J., & Meakings, S. (2013). 'Other children say you're not normal because you don't live with your parents'. Children's views of living with informal kinship carers: Social networks, stigma and attachment to carers. *Child & Family Social Work, 18*(1), 25–34.

Fernandez, E. (2009). Children's wellbeing in care: Evidence from a longitudinal study of outcomes. *Children and Youth Services Review, 31*(10), 1092–1100.

Gilligan, R. (2000). The developmental implications for children of life in public care: Irish and international perspectives. *The Irish Journal of Psychology, 21*(3–4), 138–153.

Groza, V., & Bunkers, K. M. (2017). Best practices for residential/institutional/group care of children: A harm reduction framework. In A. V. Rus, S. R. Parris, & E. Stativa (Eds.), *Child maltreatment in residential care* (pp. 477–492). Cham: Springer.

Gypen, L., Vanderfaeillie, J., De Maeyer, S., Belenger, L., & Van Holen, F. (2017). Outcomes of children who grew up in foster care: Systematic-review. *Children and Youth Services Review, 76*, 74–83.

Healey, C. V., & Fisher, P. A. (2011). Young children in foster care and the development of favorable outcomes. *Children and Youth Services Review, 33*(10), 1822–1830.

Khoo, E., Skoog, V., & Dalin, R. (2012). In and out of care: A profile and analysis of children in the out-of-home care system in Sweden. *Children and Youth Services Review, 34*(5), 900–907.

Kiraly, M., & Humphreys, C. (2016). 'It's about the whole family': Family contact for children in kinship care. *Child & Family Social Work, 21*(2), 228–239.

López, M., & del Valle, J. F. (2013). The waiting children: Pathways (and future) of children in long-term residential care. *The British Journal of Social Work, 45*(2), 457–473.

McConkey, R., Kelly, F., & Craig, S. (2012). A national comparative study over one decade of children with intellectual disabilities living away from their natural parents. *British Journal of Social Work, 44*(3), 714–728.

McEvoy, O., & Smith, M. D. (2011). *Listen to our voices! Hearing children and young people living in the care of the state*. Dublin: Government Publications.

McGhee, J., Bunting, L., McCartan, C., Elliott, M., Bywaters, P., & Featherstone, B. (2017). Looking after children in the UK – Convergence or divergence? *The British Journal of Social Work, 48*(5), 1176–1198.

McGregor, C., Lynch, M., & Brady, B. (2017). Youth mentoring as a form of support for children and young people at risk. In P. Dolan & N. Frost (Eds.), *The Routledge handbook of global child welfare* (pp. 345–357). London and New York, NY: Taylor & Francis.

McMahon, C., & Curtin, C. (2013). The social networks of young people in Ireland with experience of long-term foster care: Some lessons for policy and practice. *Child & Family Social Work, 18*(3), 329–340.

McSherry, D., Larkin, E., Fargas, M., Kelly, G. M., Robinson, C., Macdonald, G. M., ... Kilpatrick, R. (2010). *From care to where? A care pathways and outcomes report for practitioners*. Belfast: Institute for Child Care Research, Queen's University Belfast.

Mendis, K., Lehmann, J., & Gardner, F. (2017). Promoting academic success of children in care. *British Journal of Social Work, 48*(1), 106–123.

Mertz, M., & Andersen, S. H. (2017). The hidden cost of foster-care: New evidence on the inter-generational transmission of foster-care experiences. *British Journal of Social Work, 47*(5), 1377–1393.

Mollidor, C., & Berridge, D. (2017). Residential care for children and young people: Policy and practice challenges. In P. Dolan & N. Frost (Eds.), *The Routledge handbook of global child welfare* (pp. 280–292). London and New York, NY: Taylor & Francis.

Moran, L., McGregor, C., & Devaney, C. (2016). Scoping review of Irish and international literature on outcomes for permanence and stability for children in care. Dublin: Tusla, the Child and Family Agency/Galway: UNESCO Child and Family Research Centre, Galway.

Moran, L., McGregor, C., & Devaney, C. (2017). *Outcomes for permanence and stability for children in long-term care: Practice guidance*. Galway: UNESCO Child and Family Research Centre, Galway.

Mulheir, G., & Gyllensten, L. L. (2017). Institutionalization and the commodification of children: How to ensure children regain their right to family life. In P. Dolan & N. Frost (Eds.), *The Routledge handbook of global child welfare* (pp. 293–312). London and New York, NY: Taylor & Francis.

Nandy, S., & Selwyn, J. (2012). Kinship care and poverty: Using census data to examine the extent and nature of kinship care in the UK. *British Journal of Social Work, 43*(8), 1649–1666.

Napier, H. (1972). Success and failure in foster care. *The British Journal of Social Work, 2*(2), 187–204.

Petrowski, N., Cappa, C., & Gross, P. (2017). Estimating the number of children in formal alternative care: Challenges and results. *Child Abuse & Neglect, 70*, 388–398.

Pinkerton, J. (2011). Constructing a global understanding of the social ecology of leaving out of home care. *Children and Youth Services Review, 33*(12), 2412–2416.

Refaeli, T., Mangold, K., Zeira, A., & Köngeter, S. (2017). Continuity and discontinuity in the transition from care to adulthood. *The British Journal of Social Work, 47*(2), 325–342.

Roarty, N., Leinster, J., McGregor, C., & Moran, L. (2018). Outcomes for permanence and stability for children in long-term care in Ireland. *Outcomes for Permanence and Stability for Children in Long-Term Care in Ireland, 5*, 52–62.

Rock, S., Michelson, D., Thomson, S., & Day, C. (2013). Understanding foster placement instability for looked after children: A systematic review and narrative synthesis of quantitative and qualitative evidence. *British Journal of Social Work, 45*(1), 177–203.

Rogers, J. (2016). 'Different'and 'Devalued': Managing the Stigma of foster-care with the benefit of peer support. *British Journal of Social Work, 47*(4), 1078–1093.

Schofield, G., Larsson, B., & Ward, E. (2017). Risk, resilience and identity construction in the life narratives of young people leaving residential care. *Child & Family Social Work, 22*(2), 782–791.

Selwyn, J., & Riley, S. (2015). *Children and young people's views on being in care*. Bristol: University of Bristol and Coram Voices.

Sen, R. (2015). Not all that is solid melts into air? Care-experienced young people, friendship and relationships in the 'digital age'. *The British Journal of Social Work, 46*(4), 1059–1075.

Serbinski, S., & Brown, J. (2016). Creating connections with child welfare workers: Experiences of foster parents' own children. *British Journal of Social Work, 47*(5), 1411–1426.

Skoog, V., Khoo, E., & Nygren, L. (2014). Disconnection and dislocation: Relationships and belonging in unstable foster and institutional care. *The British Journal of Social Work, 45*(6), 1888–1904.

Steels, S., & Simpson, H. (2017). Perceptions of children in residential care homes: A critical review of the literature. *The British Journal of Social Work, 47*(6), 1704–1722.

Stein, M. (2008). Transitions from care to adulthood: Messages from research. In M. Stein & E. R. Munro (Eds.), *Young people's transition from care to adulthood: International research and practice.* London: Jessica Kingsley Publishers.

Stein, M. (2012). *Young people leaving care: Supporting pathways to adulthood.* London: Jessica Kingsley Publishers.

Stein, M., & Munro, E. R. (Eds.). (2008). *Young people's transitions from care to adulthood: International comparisons and perspectives.* London: Jessica Kingsley Publishers.

Sulimani-Aidan, Y. (2016). Future expectations as a source of resilience among young people leaving care. *British Journal of Social Work, 47*(4), 1111–1127.

Sutton, L., & Stack, N. (2012). Hearing quiet voices: Biological children's experiences of fostering. *British Journal of Social Work, 43*(3), 596–612.

Thoburn, J., & Ainsworth, F. (2015). Making sense of differential cross-national placement rates for therapeutic residential care: Some takeaway messages for policy. In J. K. Whittaker, J. F. del Valle, & L. Holmes (Eds.), *Therapeutic residential care with children and youth: Developing evidence-based international practice* (pp. 37–49). London: Jessica Kingsley.

Thompson, R. W., Duppong Hurley, K., Trout, A. L., Huefner, J. C., & Daly, D. L. (2017). Closing the research to practice gap in therapeutic residential care: Service provider – University partnerships focused on evidence-based practice. *Journal of Emotional and Behavioral Disorders, 25*(1), 46–56.

UNITED NATIONS. General Assembly. (2010). *Guidelines for the alternative care of children.* New York, NY: United Nations.

Vanderfaeillie, J., Van Holen, F., Vanschoonlandt, F., Robberechts, M., & Stroobants, T. (2013). Children placed in long-term family foster care: A longitudinal study into the development of problem behavior and associated factors. *Children and Youth Services Review, 35*(4), 587–593.

Whittaker, J. K. (2017). Pathways to evidence-based practice in therapeutic residential care: A commentary. *Journal of Emotional and Behavioral Disorders, 25*(1), 57–61.

Winter, K. (2012). Understanding and supporting young children's transitions into state care: Schlossberg's transition framework and child-centred practice. *British Journal of Social Work, 44*(2), 401–417.

Wright, K., Swain, S., & McPhillips, K. (2017). The Australian royal commission into institutional responses to child sexual abuse. *Child Abuse and Neglect* (Special Issue), 74, 1–114.

3 Natural and youth-initiated mentoring

3.1 Introduction

Natural mentors have been defined as 'important non-parental adults, such as teachers, coaches, neighbours and extended family members, from whom a young person receives support and guidance' (Zimmerman, Bingenheimer, & Behrendt, 2005, as cited in Horn & Spencer, 2018, p. 183). According to Greeson, Thompson, and Wegner (2015, p. 141), a natural mentor is a 'non-parental, supportive adult whom a youth self-selects from his or her existing social network'. With formal mentoring, the relationship or 'match' is facilitated by an agency, such as Big Brothers Big Sisters, whereas with natural mentoring, the relationship forms naturally and proceeds in the same 'organic' way as any naturally formed relationship (Greeson, Thompson, Evans-Chase, & Ali, 2015, p. 94). For young people in care, these natural mentoring relationships may be developed with people from their extended family, schools and neighbourhoods, but also 'the various services with which they interact, including foster carers, youth workers and social workers' (Zinn, 2017, p. 565).

In this chapter, we firstly look at the concept of natural mentoring and review some of the research findings regarding this phenomenon. We then move on to look specifically at research findings in relation to natural mentoring for children in care and the practice implications arising from these research findings are also discussed. Finally, we explore the concept of youth-initiated mentoring, a new approach that has been developed to extend the benefits of natural mentoring to a broader population of youth.

3.2 Natural mentoring

Interest in the role of natural mentors in the lives of children at risk has been growing since the publication of Werner and Smith's (1982) ground-breaking longitudinal study of children who had experienced adversity in Hawaii. They found the presence of a consistent care-giver or natural mentor to be a key factor in enabling young people to make successful transitions to adulthood, in spite of experiencing significant adversity throughout childhood and adolescence. Subsequent studies by Garmezy (1985), Rutter and Giller (1983) also drew attention to the presence of at least one non-parental adult who provides consistent support as contributing to the resilience of young people. Stanton-Salazar and Spina (2003) showed how informal mentors and role models can have an empowering influence in the lives of urban, Latino youth in California.

Since these early studies, a large body of research has shown that children and young people with a natural mentor have better outcomes in many domains than those without a mentor. For example, in a US study of 770 adolescents, Rhodes, Grossman, and Roffman (2002) found that the 52% of students surveyed who reported having a natural mentor had more positive attitudes towards school, greater school attachment and efficacy, less marijuana use and less nonviolent delinquency. Young Latina and African American mothers with natural mentors were found to have lower levels of depression than those without mentors (Rhodes, Ebert, & Fischer, 1992). Van Dam et al. (2018) conducted a meta-analytic review of 30 studies of natural mentoring conducted since 1992. They found a significant association between the presence of a natural mentor and positive youth outcomes, most notably social-emotional development and academic and vocational achievement.

Non-parental adults are seen to provide a range of roles in young people's development. They provide support, communicate and model values, foster learning and skills development and promote self-esteem (Southwick, Morgan, Vythilingam, & Charney, 2007). From a psychological perspective, mentors can serve as 'external regulators' whose capacities and strengths can be 'borrowed' until the mentee can gradually internalise them. They can provide role models for interacting with others. From a social perspective, mentors can expose young people to new environments and ways of thinking. This may lead to the development of new friendships and supportive relationships. Southwick et al. (2007) also highlight that mentoring can help to activate the 'complex neurobiological circuitry that is associated with reward, attachment, learning and memory' (p. 582). They point out that ongoing imitation of a mentor's behaviour over time can lead to the activation of new areas of the brain, the formation of new neuronal branches and connections and increases in synaptic transmission. Stanton-Salazar (2011) has also written about the importance of mentors as 'institutional agents' who provide key forms of social and institutional support to youth.

3.3 Natural mentoring for children in care

Over the past two decades in particular, research and practice attention has focused on the role of natural mentoring in the lives of children and young people in care. Much of this research has been undertaken in the United States, where a number of key studies have established the significant role that natural mentors can play in the lives of children and young people

Natural and youth-initiated mentoring   45

in care. In this section, we draw on the research evidence to answer three questions:

- How prevalent is natural mentoring and what outcomes have been associated with it?
- What are the key features or characteristics of positive natural mentoring relationships?
- What challenges are faced in forming and maintaining natural mentoring relationships?

How prevalent is natural mentoring and what outcomes have been associated with it?

There is a growing body of research showing associations between the presence of a natural mentor and well-being outcomes among children and young people in care. A meta-analysis of 38 research studies on the evidence in relation to the role of natural mentors for foster youth conducted by Thompson, Greeson, and Brunsink (2016) found that there is evidence that natural mentors play an important role in the lives of many children and young people in care, and that many studies reported a positive relationship between natural mentoring and improved psychosocial, behavioural or academic outcomes.

One of the first studies to explore the prevalence and benefits of natural mentoring for young people in care was conducted by Ahrens, DuBois, Richardson, Fan, and Lozano (2008). Drawing on data from Waves I to III of the National Longitudinal Study of Adolescent Health (1994–2002), the study explored whether young people in foster care with natural mentors during adolescence had better outcomes as a young adult. Youth were considered to have had a mentoring relationship if it began before the age of 18 years and lasted for at least two years. Of the 310 young people in foster care in the cohort, 160 were found to have had a natural mentor in their lives. Relationships were most frequently reported to be with non-parental family members (36%), such as grandparents, aunts and uncles. Just over one in five (21%) reported that their mentors were adults in professional roles such as teachers, guidance counsellors or ministers, while 11% of mentors were people the young person knew in more informal capacities (e.g. coaches, friends' parents, co-workers, friends, 11%). The average relationship duration reported was 9.7 years. The young people who had a mentor in adolescence were more likely to do better in adulthood in terms of overall health, educational attainment, physical aggression, suicide risk and risk of sexually transmitted infection than non-mentored youth. The authors conclude that while youth mentoring relationships 'cannot be expected to outweigh completely the significant risk conferred by the experience of having been in foster care, the improvements seen are clearly noteworthy in view of the poor adult outcomes seen among young in foster care' (p. 251). The authors note that the findings of their study indicate stronger outcomes than similar studies focusing on formal mentoring for youth in foster care. They speculate that the extended duration of natural mentoring relationships compared to formal mentoring relationships may have contributed to the favourable outcomes observed.

Positive outcomes were also found in a study of natural mentoring relationships among older youth in foster care in the United States by Munson and McMillen (2009). Of the 339 young people who took part, 25% ($n = 85$) reported that they had no mentor, 41% ($n = 139$) reported a short term mentor, and 34% ($n = 115$) reported a long term mentoring relationship. The authors found that the presence of a mentor and a longer relationship were associated with better psychological outcomes, such as fewer depression symptoms, less stress and more satisfaction with life. Compared to those that did not nominate a mentor, youth in long term natural mentoring relationships reported less stress and were less likely to have been arrested at age 19.

Duke, Farruggia, and Germo (2017, p. 66) define very important non-parental adults (VIPs) as those adults that 'youth identify as important and can be counted on'. They conducted survey and interview research with an ethnically diverse group of 99 young adults, who had recently transitioned from care in a large US city. These young adults reported having a very important non-parental adult (VIP) and 63 of the VIPs were also included in their study. The study found that 40% of VIP relationships emanated from pre-existing familial networks, with 78% of youth having met their VIP before adolescence. Sixty-five percent of youth indicated that their VIP provided some type of support. The relationship was described as being 'parent like', respectful and reciprocal with regards to communication. Both the youth and the VIPs viewed these relationships to be important in reducing negative outcomes for the youth. According to Duke and colleagues, the results suggest that the VIP may act as 'a buffer for the young person against a number of risky situations, including substance abuse, homelessness and imprisonment' (p. 71).

Zinn's (2017) analysis of a panel of 683 former foster care youth in the Midwest United States found that almost four-fifths (79.6%) of participating youth reported having a natural mentor at one or more of the three measurement points of the study. Among youth with natural mentors, approximately a third reported that their mentor was, respectively, a family member (39.7%) or a family acquaintance (35.1%). About a sixth (16.6%) indicated that their mentors were affiliated with a social institution like a school, religious organization or employer or with a social service agency or mentoring program (8.6%). Those whose mentors were family members or family acquaintances reported higher levels of contact and emotional closeness than other youth.

Taken together, the research findings in relation to young people in foster care suggest that natural mentoring relationships are common among children and young people in care and that the presence of these relationships is associated with positive outcomes (Greeson, Weiler, Thompson, & Taussig,

2016; Horn & Spencer, 2018). Research has also explored the characteristics of positive natural mentoring relationships.

What are the characteristics of positive natural mentoring relationships?

The nature of natural mentoring relationships can change over the period of adolescence. Extended family members are more likely to serve as mentors for younger children, whereas mentoring relationships with non-familial mentors (e.g. teacher, youth worker, sports coach) often develop during middle and later adolescence as youth gradually expand their social networks (Fruiht & Wray-Lake, 2013). While family mentoring relationships are often close, durable and strong on emotional support, older youth may also benefit from the development of weak ties or bridging social capital with non-family members that can link them to education, training or employment opportunities (Van Dam et al., 2018; Raposa, Erickson, Hagler, & Rhodes, 2018).

Munson, Smalling, Spencer, Scott, and Tracy (2010) explored the relational qualities and kinds of social support that matter to older youth ($n = 189$) nearing their exit from the foster care system. In terms of the qualities of natural mentors, the most valued personality qualities were being approachable, easy to be with, easy-going and kind. A key feature of natural mentors identified by the young people was that they were understanding. Many respondents emphasised similarities between them and their mentors as factors which enhanced their relationships – be it a similar background, having had similar experiences or interests. Young people valued that their mentors were consistent in keeping in contact, gave freely of their time and were 'always there' for them (p. 530). Trust and the mentors' commitment to confidentiality were also important. Young people also valued that the mentor was 'real' or authentic with them, listened to them, was not judgemental or condescending and created spaces in which the young people felt they could talk honestly. Many young people felt that the mentors truly understood them and the context within which they lived their lives, which in many cases was a result of them knowing each other over a long period. The fact that many mentors had shared stories of similar experiences in their own lives appeared to enhance their credibility and trustworthiness. 'The narratives of these youth suggested that they felt that the mentors could better understand them in part because they demonstrated their knowledge and awareness of the complexities inherent in their lives in the foster care system' (p. 531).

Munson et al. (2010) also explored the nature of support provided by mentors. For many young people, their mentor was someone who helped to keep them 'on track' and was not afraid to offer honest feedback and hold the young person accountable for their behaviour. Mentors also provided concrete or tangible support, including childcare, housing and financial support and helping the young person to find a job. Information or advice support was also valued; again this could relate to employment or educational choices but also to peer and intimate relationships. In terms of emotional support, young people spoke of mentors listening and helping them with emotionally difficult issues and helping them to understand them more clearly.

Similar themes emerged in a study undertaken by Ahrens et al. (2011), which involved interviews with 23 young people aged 18 to 25 who had previously been in foster care regarding their relationships with non-parental adults. The factors that helped to facilitate a connection developing included the mentor being patient but persistent, showing that s/he cared rather than leaving the young person when things got tough. Authentic displays of support were seen as critical, such as the mentor sharing his or her own experience and going beyond the confines of the 'prescribed relationship' (p. 1016). In keeping with the broader mentoring literature, they also found that having interests or characteristics in common was important. On the practical side, the relationship was helped by having mechanisms in place to maintain regular contact. In line with the Rhodes model of youth mentoring (2005), they found that mentors helped young people in the following ways:

- Socio-emotional development: Mentors helped young people with dealing with conflict, managing anger, looking after themselves and setting boundaries in their relationships.
- Cognitive development: By engaging in conversation with mentors, young people described how they were challenged to think through the pros and cons of situations. Young people spoke of developing independent living skills, such as cooking, driving and budgeting.
- Identity development: Mentors helped young people to improve their self-worth and to counter some of the negative messages they may have received in this regard. Mentors were also seen to link young people with opportunities for progression.

Characteristics of natural mentors

Easy-going
Kind
Understanding
Approachable
Non-judgemental
Authentic or 'real'
Respectful
Reciprocal
Similar backgrounds
Experience of adversity
Similar interests
Patient but persistent

What challenges are faced in forming and maintaining natural mentoring relationships?

While a large number of young people have reported natural mentoring relationships, a significant number of young people do not have such potentially beneficial relationships in their lives. Studies have highlighted some of the issues or barriers that young people can face in establishing or maintaining natural mentoring relationships. Frequent disruption and changes of placement can mean that young people are moved from schools, neighbourhoods and communities where they have developed strong connections and possibly natural mentoring relationships (Horn & Spencer, 2018). Young people participating in research by Munson et al. (2010) described a range of practical or logistical barriers that made it difficult to maintain natural mentoring relationships, including moving placement, the mentor moving away and loss of contact information. Emotional barriers were also identified, with some young people speaking of their fears that they would get hurt if they became close to the mentor and/or that the mentor would fail them in some way. Others felt that they would feel a sense of indebtedness to the mentor that they might not be in a position to repay. Other concerns were that the mentor would not understand their background, that they would 'tell' them what to do. Some young people felt that they hadn't lived up to the mentors' expectations so were reluctant to meet with them and risk disappointing them.

Similarly, some young people taking part in research by Greeson et al. (2015) said that they felt insecure about other people's perceptions of them as a result of their life history and possibly being viewed as 'deviant', expressing a preference for a mentor who they did not previously know and who can 'start from scratch' and 'can't pre-judge you' (p. 144). Other young people spoke of the difficulties associated with filling the voids left by the absence of key adults in their lives, such as a father figure.

What are the implications for practice from the research on natural mentors?

Researchers have made a number of recommendations regarding how natural mentoring for children in care can be better supported in practice.

Supporting the development of natural mentoring relationships: Horn and Spencer (2018) highlight that many barriers to the development of natural mentoring relationships exist at the service level, including placement disruption which means that young people may lose touch with people to whom they have become close. They argue that avoiding placement disruption can provide opportunities for youth to develop and maintain important relationships. They also highlight that a high turnover in staff in child welfare agencies can have a negative impact on the quality of relationships that are developed between these adults and children/young people. Horn and Spencer (2018, p. 229) argue 'because these relationships are models for how youth perceive relationships with other adults, more care should be taken in preventing unnecessary worker transition for youth in care'.

Mentor recruitment: The research on natural mentoring has shown that young people value mentors who have had similar life experiences to them, particularly those that have had some experience of the care system (Ahrens et al., 2011; Munson et al., 2010). Munson et al. (2010) speculate that having had similar difficult experiences may help to reduce shame and lead to young people 'bringing more of themselves into the relationships' (p. 533). They argue that organisations working with youth leaving foster care should look carefully at ways of supporting existing natural mentoring relationships, rather than trying to create new ones with adults who may not share some of the life experiences and characteristics that have been identified as important by youth.

The literature also emphasises that mentors with specific training as helping professionals may have the skills to bond effectively with difficult and/or resistant youth. Ahrens et al. (2011) found that young people often discussed relationships with adults they had met through the child welfare system as being of particular importance, indicating that this may be a particular source of support for young people in care. There is a growing body of evidence that youth mentoring relationships are more beneficial when the mentor has experience in helping roles or professions (e.g. teacher, counsellor, social worker, therapist) (Jarjoura, Tanyu, Forbush, Herrera, & Keller, 2018; Raposa et al., 2018; Rhodes, 2018; Van Dam et al., 2018).

One of the striking features of the research on natural mentoring is the importance of long-term relationships to support the young person through the multiple adversities and transitions that they faced in their lives. Because older young people leaving foster care have often had many moves in their lives, 'the consistent presence of a trusted and caring adult over the course of these many transitions may be especially meaningful to them' (Munson et al., 2010, p. 533). This finding has implications for formal mentoring programmes. While many formal mentoring relationships can endure for many years, the standard one year commitment required by formal mentoring programmes may not be sufficient to provide the long-term support that is needed by young people in care.

Support youth to identify mentors: Approximately half of young people in foster care report the absence of a relationship with a caring adult (Ahrens et al., 2008; Greeson, Usher, & Grinstein-Weiss, 2010). Given the potential benefits associated with natural mentors, it has been suggested that it may be useful to offer training and support to youth in foster care to help them to recognise and cultivate relationships with non-parental adults (Ahrens et al., 2011; Duke et al., 2017; Zinn, 2017). While many emphasise training youth to identify and build connections with suitable adults, Zinn (2017) suggested that ongoing behavioural and emotional supports and strategies to help youth build social and emotional skills may also be important in helping youth to connect with natural mentors and ensure that these mentor relationships are positive and impactful. Some youth-initiated mentoring models have been developed for this purpose and will be reviewed later in this chapter.

Training for mentors: Ahrens et al. (2011) also argue that it may be worthwhile to develop training specifically for mentors of young people in foster care that incorporates learning from research on the factors that influence relationship quality and duration for this group of young people. They believe that this could help to raise awareness of the challenges faced by young people and highlight potential strategies to deal with any issues that may arise.

Incorporate a focus on mentoring in care and permanency planning: A number of authors have recommended that a greater focus on mentoring be incorporated into care and permanency planning (Avery, 2010; Horn & Spencer, 2018). Horn and Spencer (2018) suggest that it may be useful to include natural mentors more formally in planning for the young person leaving care on the basis that they may have 'unique insights' into the young person's needs and may be able to offer ongoing support to help them to meet their goals. They also make the point that where the mentor previously had a formal role in the young person's life, including them in the planning process would allow them to be involved 'without overstepping professional boundaries', which was expressed as a concern for some mentors (p. 1021).

There is an emphasis within legislation on permanency planning for children in care, which is generally understood as connecting young people to adoptive families and other kinship arrangements. Horn and Spencer (2018) argue that while these strategies may be ideal for younger children and children likely to reunify with family, they may be less effective for older youth who are unlikely to be adopted or to reunify with family. As an alternative, they and Greeson (2013) argue that more funding should be given to youth mentoring organisations focusing on natural mentoring support to support young people to develop high quality relationships in the transition to adulthood.

According to Greeson et al. (2015), studies have shown that many young people see the relational or emotional aspects of permanence are more important than the legal or physical, leading to a focus on the concept of 'relational permanence' as an additional way to conceptualise the meaning of permanence (Freundlich, Avery, Munson, & Gerstenzang, 2006). Relational permanence has been defined by Jones and LaLiberte (2013, p. 509) as 'youth experiencing a sense of belonging through enduring life-long connections to parents, extended family or other caring adults, including at least one adult who will provide a permanent, parent-like connection for that youth'. Relationships with natural mentors are considered to be a form of relational permanence.

3.4 Youth-initiated mentoring

Youth-initiated mentoring (YIM) is a new approach that brings together aspects of formal and natural mentoring. Rather than being assigned a mentor, young people are supported to recruit caring adults from within their own networks (e.g. relative, neighbour or friend). The nominated adult is asked if he or she is willing to act as an informal mentor for the young person. When the mentoring relationship is formally established, mentors and youth are expected to meet regularly over an extended period of time, typically for a year. As with formal mentoring programmes, support for the match, including goal setting and trouble-shooting, is provided by the mentoring organisation. The goal of youth-initiated mentoring is similar to formal mentoring: namely to support the young person to deal with challenges in his or her life and to become more resilient.

The attraction of this approach, according to Spencer, Tugenberg, Ocean, Schwartz, and Rhodes (2016, p. 403), is that it brings 'the intuitive appeal of formalising existing connections with adults in youths' own communities'. This practice is in keeping with strengths based approaches which draw on the strengths and potential of natural social networks, acknowledging that professionally based interventions have limitations (Van Dam et al., 2017). By recruiting a mentor from the young person's own social network, it is envisaged that the mentoring relationship will not take so long to develop and will be more sustainable in the long term than one created through a formal mentoring programme. Spencer et al. (2016, p. 404) make the point that the mentors selected by the young people 'may have a higher level of investment in their protégés' and 'may also be less prone to the disappointments and dashed expectations experienced by some mentors in more traditional programs'. Because the mentors are more likely to be from backgrounds which are similar to those of the young person, they may represent more realistic or meaningful role models than a mentor from a different background that the young person finds it harder to identify with. Spencer et al. (2016) also point out that YIM can help to eliminate the long waiting lists youth experience in many formal mentoring programs due to difficulties recruiting sufficient numbers of volunteer mentors. Horn and Spencer (2018, p. 230) see the encouragement of 'youth voice and choice' as especially important for young people in foster care as these young people are often tired and disappointed from previous relationship experiences and wary at the prospect of forming new relationships with adults.

Practice example: real connections

Foster Forward in Rhode Island, United States, is a voluntary organization dedicated to supporting children, young adults, and families whose lives have been impacted by foster care. Their Real Connections Program connects foster youth, ages 8–21, with positive, long-lasting adult role models who can provide guidance and emotional support. The young people are supported to identify and forge meaningful connections with trusted adults. The programme then facilitates and support these mentoring relationships, tailoring the program to each young person's needs and goals. More information about the programme can be found via the following Internet links:

www.fosterforward.net/programs-initiatives/for-children-teens/real-connections-mentor-program/
https://chronicle.umbmentoring.org/profiles-in-mentoring-program-coordinator-kate-bronner/

What benefits have been associated with youth-initiated mentoring?

Youth-initiated mentoring is a relatively new approach and thus the evidence base is small but growing. A small number of studies have examined the benefits of the YIM approach with young people in care.

Van Dam et al. (2017) compared the case files of 96 young people who took part in a YIM programme in the Netherlands with the case files of 104 young people in residential care. A total of 83% of young people were able to nominate an informal mentor from their social network, on average within 33 days. The profile of mentors nominated by youth included family members (43%), a friend (17%), a friend of their parents (12%), an acquaintance (11%), a neighbour (5%) and another person (e.g. teacher, sports coach) (12%). Social and emotional support was the most common type of support offered, followed by practical support, guidance and advice.

The majority of young people participating in the youth-initiated mentoring programme would otherwise have been allocated to an out-of-home placement. An individualised care package was developed for each young person, which consisted of discussions with the mentor and additional supports such as therapy, instrumental support and education. An out-of-home placement was considered necessary for eight adolescents (10%), including placement in a psychiatric crisis residential facility or a kinship or non-kinship foster-care family. Based on the findings of this small scale study, the authors believe that that the YIM approach may offer a viable alternative to out-of-home placement. At the time of writing in 2017, the YIM approach had been implemented by 22 mental health care organisations in the Netherlands.

Spencer, Gowdy, Drew, and Rhodes (2019) undertook a qualitative study with mentors, youth and parents/guardians to explore their perceptions of the youth-initiated mentoring programme for children and young people involved with social services. In line with other studies of YIM, they found that young people were able to identify appropriate adults to serve as mentors. The YIM approach built on the young person's previous feelings of trust in the mentor and ensured that the relationship could become established more quickly, 'skipping over what can be an extended, potentially awkward "getting to know you phase" in traditionally matched pairs' (p. 21). Mentors were found to value the fact that they were chosen by the young person, which enhanced their commitment to the mentoring relationship. Interestingly, mentors all said that they would have been unlikely to sign up to a mentoring programme if they had not been asked by the young person. Spencer et al. (2019) suggest that YIM programmes have the capacity to 'tap into a different pool of adult mentors than is being reached through current recruitment efforts' (p. 19). Furthermore, because mentors were chosen specifically for this role, their main motivation was to offer support to the young person who nominated them. This is in contrast to the situation in more general mentoring programmes, where the mentors' motivation for volunteering can vary and include selfish motives.

Challenges associated with youth-initiated mentoring

Some of the challenges associated with youth-initiated mentoring have also been noted in the literature. Some young people may not have appropriate adults that they can nominate as mentors or may be unwilling to do so (Greeson et al., 2015). Mentors may be unable to take up the role for various reasons, including time constraints. Another challenge relates to bonding and bridging social capital – if mentors are too similar to young people, they may not be able to connect the young person with resources and social connections outside of their own communities to help them to get ahead (Spencer et al., 2016).

While YIM is seen as a potentially valuable approach for young people in care, more evaluation research is needed of programmes that adopt YIM approaches with children in care (Horn & Spencer, 2018).

Web resources

> Youth Initiated Mentoring (YIM) www.youtube.com/watch?v=4mBw_1HZiBc&feature=youtu.be
>
> https://chronicle.umbmentoring.org/three-new-studies-studies-on-youth-initiated-mentoring/

3.5 Conclusion

This chapter has reviewed existing literature relating to natural mentoring. We have explained what this means and how best it can work for young people. The evidence is strong to support the value of having one supportive non-parenting adult especially when that relationship is sustained over time. The challenges to maintaining natural mentor relationships for children in care however are significant. They can be practical in that the young person moves to a different location. They can be emotional in that the complexity of the issues for the young person may be too intense or difficult for a natural mentor to manage if they do not have a background themselves in supportive work with young people. The idea of youth-initiated mentoring has significant merit and it would seem that there is high value in building the identification of the 'one supportive adult' into the formal care planning process more explicitly. As we come towards the end of the chapter, the link between natural and formal mentoring is discussed and some of the issues are common. For example, when we discuss implications for practice, in some ways, the suggestion seems to be that we formalise natural mentoring through integration into planning, training, support and resourcing. While this is an important feature, and one we talk about more as the book progresses, we would emphasise the importance of not trying to over-formalise the potential of natural mentoring either as this runs counter to its very definition and meaning as discussed at the beginning.

Summary points: natural mentoring relationships

- Natural mentoring relationships are drawn from the young person's own social network and thus tend to last longer and be seen as more meaningful by the young people.
- Some studies include natural mentors who are family while others focus on non-family members only.
- Studies have found that young people in care with natural mentors have better outcomes in a range of areas compared to young people without a mentor.
- Non-parental adults can provide a range of roles in young people's development, including support, modelling of values, fostering learning and skills development and the promotion of self-esteem.
- Trust and authenticity are key features of natural mentoring relationships.
- Many studies conclude that intervention efforts should focus on cultivating mentoring relationships within the existing social networks of young people in foster care rather than assigning mentors through formal programmes. Youth-initiated mentoring is a relatively new approach that aims to do this.
- A small number of studies have examined the benefits of the YIM approach with young people in care and found it to be a promising approach.

References

Ahrens, K. R., Dubois, D. L., Garrison, M., Spencer, R., Richardson, L. P., & Lozano, P. (2011). Qualitative exploration of relationships with important non-parental adults in the lives of youth in foster care. *Children and Youth Services Review, 33*(6), 1012–1023.

Ahrens, K. R., Dubois, D. L., Richardson, L. P., Fan, M. Y., & Lozano, P. (2008). Youth in foster care with adult mentors during adolescence have improved adult outcomes. *Pediatrics, 121*(2), 246–252.

Avery, R. J. (2010). An examination of theory and promising practice for achieving permanency for teens before they age out of foster care. *Children and Youth Services Review, 32*(3), 399–408.

Duke, T., Farruggia, S. P., & Germo, G. R. (2017). "I don't know where I would be right now if it wasn't for them": Emancipated foster care youth and their important non-parental adults. *Children and Youth Services Review, 76*, 65–73.

Freundlich, M., Avery, R. J., Munson, S., & Gerstenzang, S. (2006). The meaning of permanency in child welfare: Multiple stakeholder perspectives. *Children and Youth Services Review, 28*(7), 741–760.

Fruiht, V. M., & Wray-Lake, L. (2013). The role of mentor type and timing in predicting educational attainment. *Journal of Youth and Adolescence, 42*(9), 1459–1472.

Garmezy, N. (1985). Stress-resistant children: The search for protective factors. *Recent Research in Developmental Psychopathology, 4*, 213–233.

Greeson, J. K. (2013). Foster youth and the transition to adulthood: The theoretical and conceptual basis for natural mentoring. *Emerging Adulthood, 1*(1), 40–51.

Greeson, J. K. P., Thompson, A. E., Evans-Chase, M., & Ali, S. (2015). Welfare professionals' attitudes and beliefs about child welfare-based natural mentoring for older youth in foster care. *Journal of Social Service Research, 41*(1), 93–112.

Greeson, J. K. P., Thompson, A. E., & Wenger, R. S. (2015). It's good to know that you got somebody that's not going anywhere: Attitudes and beliefs of older youth in foster care about child welfare-based natural mentoring. *Children and Youth Services Review, 48*, 140–149.

Greeson, J. K. P., Usher, L., & Grinstein-Weiss, M. (2010). One adult who is crazy about you: Can natural mentoring relationships increase assets among young adults with and without foster care experience? *Children and Youth Services Review, 32*(4), 565–577.

Greeson, J. K. P., Weiler, L. M., Thompson, A. E., & Taussig, H. N. (2016). A first look at natural mentoring among preadolescent foster children. *Journal of Community Psychology, 44*(5), 586–601.

Horn, J. P., & Spencer, R. (2018). Natural mentoring to support the establishment of permanency for youth in foster care. *Handbook of foster youth* (p. 173). New York, NY: Routledge.

Jarjoura, G. R., Tanyu, M., Forbush, J., Herrera, C., & Keller, T. E. (2018). *Enhancement demonstration program: Technical report*. Washington, DC: American Institutes for Research.

Jones, A. S., & LaLiberte, T. (2013). Measuring youth connections: A component of relational permanence for foster youth. *Children and Youth Services Review, 35*(3), 509–517.

Munson, M. R., & McMillen, J. C. (2009). Natural mentoring and psychosocial outcomes among older youth transitioning from foster care. *Children and Youth Services Review, 31*(1), 104–111.

Munson, M. R., Smalling, S. E., Spencer, R., Scott, L. D. Jr., & Tracy, E. M. (2010). A steady presence in the midst of change: Non-kin natural mentors in the lives of older youth exiting foster care. *Children and Youth Services Review*, *32*(4), 527–535.

Raposa, E. B., Erickson, L. D., Hagler, M., & Rhodes, J. E. (2018). How economic disadvantage affects the availability and nature of mentoring relationships during the transition to adulthood. *American Journal of Community Psychology*, *61*(1–2), 191–203.

Rhodes, J. E. (2005). A model of youth mentoring. *Handbook of youth mentoring* (pp. 30–43). Thousand Oaks, CA: Sage.

Rhodes, J. E. (2018). *The loudest signal in the noise: Acknowledging a remarkably consistent finding in youth mentoring*. Retrieved from www.evidencebasedmentoring.org/the-loudest-signal-in-the-noise-a-remarkably-consistent-finding-in-youth-mentoring/

Rhodes, J. E., Ebert, L., & Fischer, K. (1992). Natural mentors: An overlooked resource in the social networks of young, African American mothers. *American Journal of Community Psychology*, *20*(4), 445–461.

Rhodes, J. E., Grossman, J. B., & Roffman, J. (2002). The rhetoric and reality of youth mentoring. *New Directions for Youth Development*, *2002*(93), 9–20.

Rutter, M., & Giller, H. (1983). *Juvenile delinquency: Trends and perspectives*. New York, NY: Guilford Publications.

Southwick, S. M., Morgan III, C. A., Vythilingam, M., & Charney, D. (2007). Mentors enhance resilience in at-risk children and adolescents. *Psychoanalytic Inquiry*, *26*(4), 577–584.

Spencer, R., Gowdy, G., Drew, A. L., & Rhodes, J. E. (2019). "Who knows me the best and can encourage me the most?": Matching and early relationship development in youth-initiated mentoring relationships with system-involved youth. *Journal of Adolescent Research*, *34*(1), 3–29.

Spencer, R., Tugenberg, T., Ocean, M., Schwartz, S. E., & Rhodes, J. E. (2016). Somebody who was on my side: A qualitative examination of youth initiated mentoring. *Youth & Society*, *48*(3), 102–124.

Stanton-Salazar, R. D. (2011). A social capital framework for the study of institutional agents and their role in the empowerment of low-status students and youth. *Youth & Society*, *43*(3), 1066–1109.

Stanton-Salazar, R. D., & Spina, S. U. (2003). Informal mentors and role models in the lives of urban Mexican-origin adolescents. *Anthropology & Education Quarterly*, *34*(3), 231–254.

Thompson, A. E., Greeson, J. K. P., & Brunsink, A. M. (2016). Natural mentoring among older youth in and aging out of foster care: A systematic review. *Children and Youth Services Review*, *61*, 40–50.

Van Dam, L., Neels, S., De Winter, M., Branje, S., Wijsbroek, S., Hutschemaekers, G., . . . Stams, G. J. J. M. (2017). Youth initiated mentors: Do they offer an alternative for out-of-home placement in youth care? *British Journal of Social Work*, *47*, 1764–1780.

Van Dam, L., Smit, D., Wildschut, B., Branje, S. J. T., Rhodes, J. E., Assink, M., & Stams, G. J. J. M. (2018). Does natural mentoring matter? A multilevel meta-analysis on the association between natural mentoring and youth outcomes. *American Journal of Community Psychology*, *62*(1–2), 203–220.

Werner, E. E., & Smith, S. (1982). *Vulnerable but invincible: A study of resilient children*. New York, NY: McGraw-Hill Companies.

Zinn, A. (2017). Predictors of natural mentoring relationships among former foster youth. *Children and Youth Services Review*, *79*, 564–575.

4 Formal youth mentoring for children in care and leaving care

4.1 Introduction

The research on natural mentoring highlights the beneficial outcomes that are associated with such relationships. However, because not all young people have natural mentors, formal mentoring programmes have been established to facilitate the formation of mentoring relationships between volunteer non-parental adults and young people. Formal mentoring programmes are based on the belief that positive relationships with adults can support young people in their emotional, cognitive and identity development into adulthood (Rhodes, 2005; Allen & Eby, 2011). Mentoring programmes typically recruit and train adult volunteers and match them with young people who are deemed to benefit from a relationship with a non-parental adult. While expectations vary according to the programme type, the mentoring pair is expected to meet weekly for a year or more. During this time, the 'match' is supported by caseworkers from the mentoring programme who ensure that both the young person and mentor are satisfied with the relationship and assist in troubleshooting if any problems arise.

While youth mentoring has been in existence for over a century in the United States, there has been a strong growth in the number of youth mentoring programmes both in the Unites States and worldwide over the past three decades (Matz, 2013).

In this chapter, we briefly review the research evidence on formal youth mentoring before moving on to focus specifically on research findings related to youth mentoring for children in care.

4.2 Research evidence in relation to formal youth mentoring

Alongside the growth of youth mentoring practice, there has been a parallel increase in mentoring research exploring the outcomes and processes associated with formal youth mentoring programmes. A series of meta-analyses of youth mentoring programme evaluations has found consistent evidence that formal youth mentoring programmes can result in positive developmental outcomes for young people (DuBois, Holloway, Valentine, & Cooper, 2002;

2011; Raposa et al., 2019). The most recent meta-analysis of 70 outcome studies of one-on-one youth mentoring programmes concluded that youth mentoring is a modestly effective intervention for youth at-risk for a range of psychosocial and academic problems (Raposa et al., 2019b; Rhodes, 2019b). Evaluations of youth mentoring programmes have reported gains in four key domains in particular.

Firstly, there is evidence that formal youth mentoring programmes can enhance emotional and psychological well-being among young people, with studies reporting outcomes including greater life satisfaction, hopefulness and reduced anxiety and depression (Barry, Clarke, Morreale, & Field, 2018; Cavell & Elledge, 2014; Dolan et al., 2011; DuBois et al., 2002; Erdem, DuBois, Larose, De Wit, & Lipman, 2016; Larsson, Pettersson, Skoog, & Erickson, 2016; Lipman, De Wit, DuBois, Larose, & Erdem, 2018; Meyerson, 2013).

Secondly, evidence of improved social relationships and skills has been found in a number of studies (De Wit, DuBois, Erdem, Larose, & Lipman, 2016; DuBois et al., 2002). For example, Chapman, Deane, Harré, Courtney, and Moore (2017) found that young people taking part in a mentoring programme had an enhanced sense of community and social self-efficacy, while improved peer and parent relationships/attachment among young people has been reported in a range of studies (Aseltine, Dupre, & Lamlein, 2000; Deane, Harre, Moore, & Courtney, 2016; Grossman & Tierney, 1998; Herrera, Grossman, Kauh, Feldman, & McMaken, 2007; Matz, 2013). Philip and Spratt's (2007) review of published UK research on mentoring and befriending found that young people who developed meaningful relationships with their mentors reported increased confidence, social support and involvement with their communities. For many young people, this relationship was a positive alternative to other relationships with family and professionals and was used as a means of re-negotiating difficult relationships with family and friends.

Thirdly, a range of studies have shown that young people who participate in mentoring programmes are less likely to engage in problem behaviour, including aggression and substance abuse (Jolliffe & Farrington, 2007; Kaplan, Skolnik, & Turnbull, 2009; Karcher & Nakkula, 2010; Tolan, Henry, Schoeny, Lovegrove, & Nichols, 2014; Williams, 2011). For example, a meta-analysis of 46 studies of mentoring programmes found that mentoring has positive effects for young people at risk of delinquency in the areas of aggression, drug use and academic performance (Tolan et al., 2014).

Fourthly, some studies have found that mentoring has led to improved educational outcomes, including staying in education for longer, better school attendance and better academic grades (Herrera et al., 2007; Matz, 2013; Simões & Alarcão, 2014). For example, in recent years, there has been a significant growth in mentoring programs in Europe to support immigrant young people to develop community bonds and to realise their potential in the education system (Crul & Schneider, 2014). Gelis (2015) researched the impact of the Nightingale Project, a social mentoring project whose aim is to support the welcoming and social inclusion of adolescent students of foreign origin who recently arrived in Catalonia and who are currently enrolled in the country's schools. After six months of mentoring, results showed that, compared to those of a similar profile who did not take part in the mentoring programme, students who participated in mentoring had learned the language faster, had broader and more diverse networks of friends in school, developed higher educational aspirations and expectations and were better acquainted with the municipality they lived in.

It is clear from the current body of research that mentoring relationships are more likely to result in positive outcomes if they implement evidence-based program practices (Kupersmidt, Stump, Stelter, & Rhodes, 2017; Raposa et al., 2019). Some of the practices and characteristics associated with more positive outcomes in youth mentoring relationships and programmes are as follows:

A close and trusting relationship: The mentoring literature strongly supports the contention that a close and trusting relationship is an essential ingredient in youth mentoring relationships. According to Rhodes (2005), positive outcomes only become possible if a meaningful relationship develops between the mentor and mentee; a 'strong interpersonal connection, characterized by mutuality, trust and empathy' (p. 31). Programmes should therefore support, encourage and nurture the development of close and trusting relationships between mentors and mentees.

Matching based on similar interests: Because a strong, close relationship is the foundation on which any positive benefits will accrue, mentors and mentees should be matched based on similar interests and compatibility. DuBois, Portillo, Rhodes, Silverthorn, and Valentine's (2011) meta-analysis found that programmes which matched mentors and youth based on similar interests produced larger effect sizes, on a variety of outcomes, than those that did not.

Mentors and mentees meet frequently: DuBois et al. (2002) found that programmes that set expectations for frequent contact between mentors and mentees showed larger effects than programmes that did not include this expectation. However, Raposa et al. (2019) caution that programmes should avoid over-burdening their mentors and mentees with expectations for lengthy meetings. Their meta-analysis found that mentoring programmes that had expectations for longer match meeting times actually yielded smaller effect sizes (Rhodes, 2019b).

Mentor training: The quality of the training and support that mentors receive has been found to play a critical role in influencing the success of youth mentoring programmes (Deutsch & Spencer, 2009; DuBois et al., 2011; Durlak & DuPre, 2008; Erdem et al., 2016; Spencer,

Basualdo-Delmonico, Walsh, & Drew, 2017). In their meta-analysis of over 55 youth mentoring programmes, DuBois et al. (2002) noted that the strength of programme effects appeared to increase dramatically when mentors were provided with ongoing training and support.

Mentor backgrounds: It is increasingly being found that mentors who work in or have previous experience in helping professions are more effective mentors (DuBois et al. 2002; Raposa et al., 2019). It is hypothesised that mentors with experience of working with young people may feel a stronger sense of efficacy and a willingness to stick with the young person in the face of difficulty than mentors without such experience (Raposa, Rhodes, & Herrera, 2016).

Mentoring styles: A body of research evidence draws our attention to the fact that some styles of mentoring may be more effective than others. Achieving a good balance between flexibility, responsiveness and structure is important; overly prescriptive mentoring styles tend to alienate young people who respond better to more equal styles (Morrow & Styles, 1995; Karcher & Nakkula, 2010; Keller & Pryce, 2012; Matz, 2013). According to DuBois and Keller (2017), mentors appear to have the most positive impact when they are able to facilitate activities that are both engaging and responsive to the interests of the mentee, but also incorporate structure and guidance to support the young person's growth and development.

4.3 Limitations and challenges associated with formal youth mentoring

While research findings show that mentoring can be a valuable intervention for young people at risk, it is important to note that the academic literature has also drawn attention to a range of challenges or limitations associated with youth mentoring as an intervention.

Limitations to the evidence base: While positive effects have been reported for youth mentoring programmes across a range of domains, the effect sizes (i.e. magnitude of change) reported in evaluations tend to be moderate (Herrera et al., 2007; De Wit, DuBois, Erdem, Larose, Lipman & Spencer, 2016; DuBois et al., 2002; DuBois et al., 2011; Erdem et al., 2016; Jolliffe & Farrington, 2007; Raposa et al., 2019). Furthermore, consistent findings are not always reported across different study evaluations (De Wit et al., 2016), which makes it difficult to generalise. In addition, a number of longitudinal evaluations which initially found positive effects found that these effects had dissipated in the period after the programme ended (Herrera, Grossman, Kauh, & McMaken, 2011; Holt, Bry, & Johnson, 2008; Karcher & Herrera, 2007; Rodriguez-Planas, 2012).

Early match closure: A key issue faced in youth mentoring programmes is maintaining relationships between mentors and mentees for the required duration (Rhodes, 2019b). De Wit et al. (2016) estimate that 30–50% of all formal youth mentoring relationships end before the standard period of commitment (typically 12 months). Research has shown that when mentoring relationships close early or unexpectedly, youth may be at increased risk of experiencing harmful behavioural, emotional or social outcomes (Kupersmidt et al., 2017). For example, Grossman and Rhodes's (2002) research found that youth whose relationships were terminated within six months suffered declines in feelings of self-worth and perceived scholastic competence, while relationships that lasted over a year had the most positive effects.

While the breakdown of some relationships is unavoidable due to changing life circumstances on the part of either mentor or mentee (MacCallum, Beltman, Coffey, & Cooper, 2014; De Wit et al., 2016), research has identified a range of programme or relationship related reasons for early match closure. In a qualitative study with mentors and mentees in a community based mentoring program whose relationships ended early, Renee Spencer (2007) identified unfulfilled expectations on the part of mentor or mentee, family interference and inadequate agency support as among the factors that contributed to early match closure. In a quantitative examination of the reasons for mentoring relationship closures among 569 youth participating in Big Brothers Big Sisters community mentoring programmes, 34% of which ended before the 12 month period of commitment, De Wit et al. (2016) found that the quality of the mentoring relationship had the strongest association with the possibility of an early match closure, whereby youth in mentoring relationships classified as high in quality experienced a reduced chance of an early closure compared to those in low to moderate quality relationships.

Based on these study findings, strategies to prevent the breakdown of youth mentoring relationships include adequate mentor training, supervision and support, diligent selection and matching processes and ongoing mentor (and mentee) support and supervision by case workers (MacCallum et al., 2014; Spencer, 2007; De Wit et al., 2016).

Recruitment of volunteers: Mentoring programmes rely on the recruitment of an adequate number of volunteers to match with young people. It is also necessary to have a pool of potential volunteers available to ensure that adults and youth can be matched based on interests and compatibility. In some mentoring programmes, difficulties in the recruitment of suitable volunteers mean that young people often have to wait for one to two years before being matched (Spencer et al., 2019). The recruitment of volunteers to act as mentors for young people can be more difficult in countries where mentoring is not so culturally ingrained as it is in the United States. For example, Brady and Curtin (2012) described how the BBBS programme was introduced to Ireland at a time when child protection issues were high in the public consciousness. The male volunteers interviewed spoke of concerns about how their involvement in the programme might be perceived by other people and referred to the fact that other people questioned why they became involved with a young person on a one-to-one basis. Challenges in the recruitment of male volunteers were acknowledged to be a factor in the lack of success of the BBBS model in the United Kingdom (Miller, 2007). Because suitable volunteers have to be found for each young person, Walker (2005) argues that the scale of mentoring will always fall short of demand (Walker, 2005).

Funding and sustainability: The majority of youth mentoring programmes are provided by non-governmental organisations and, while they may receive government funding, are generally not considered 'mainstream' social policy in the way that social work services or mental health services are, for example. Youth mentoring programme providers therefore face a range of challenges in securing ongoing funding. In a qualitative study of the wider context of youth mentoring programme delivery in the United Kingdom, Busse, Campbell, and Kipping (2018, p. 105) found that guaranteeing the sustainability of mentoring programmes seemed to be a 'juggling act' for many mentoring providers, with the result that many programmes 'hang by a thread'.

Youth mentoring and social justice: A number of authors have called for more critical reflection on how formal mentoring is understood, implemented and evaluated. Philip and Hendry (2000) argue that there is a developmental and functionalist agenda behind much of the US literature on mentoring which sees the model as a mechanism to encourage youth 'at risk' to become successful in mainstream society. They argue that there is an assumption that there is a commonly agreed standard to be reached and that the question of standards is unproblematic. This approach implicitly 'blames the victim' rather than examining the structures which inhibit young people from reaching their potential. Albright, Hurd, and Hussain (2017) argue that youth mentoring interventions hold the potential to reproduce rather than reduce inequality and that there is a need for greater attention to principles of social justice in the design, implementation and evaluation of youth mentoring interventions. Drawing on Positive Youth Development theory and community psychology, Liang, Spencer, West, and Rappaport (2013, p. 258) have proposed a shift in the mentoring field, 'from a "therapeutic" approach in which individual youth are the targets of the intervention to a more socially transformative approach wherein mentors and youth forge collaborative partnerships that promote positive youth development at individual and societal levels'.

Some authors have also argued for a broader approach to the evaluation of youth mentoring models. For example, Prieto-Flores and Gelis (2018) point out that the majority of youth mentoring research has been undertaken from a clinical or developmental psychology perspective, focusing on the outcomes of individual mentoring programmes. They argue for a more inter-disciplinary approach to mentoring research on the basis that 'we do not yet have much information on the effects of mentoring in promoting greater social justice, in combating discrimination, in participation in community social activities, or in promoting acts of service to the community, among others' (Prieto- Flores & Gelis, 2018, p. 151). In a similar vein, Philip and Spratt (2007) argue that the outcomes prioritised from mentoring programmes for children living in disadvantaged circumstances are often measured in terms of top down 'moving up and moving out' indicators, which can lead us to overlook the 'horizontal' gains that might be achieved through mentoring. For example, in qualitative studies, young people often refer to better relationships with parents or siblings as the main benefits from mentoring but these may not be picked up where 'top down' indicators of success are identified. In this regard Prieto-Flores and Gelis (2018, p. 155) note the dominance of the quantitative research, particularly experimental designs, in youth mentoring research and argue that qualitative and mixed methods studies are required in order to 'see what substantive changes social mentoring has produced in the lives of its participants, what epiphanies were experienced by participants, and what the meaning of the relationship is that was created within the framework of the program over time ... to capture a richness that, otherwise, is not collected'.

4.4 Research on formal mentoring for children in care

Formal mentoring programmes for children and young people in care can take a number of different forms. They may be general mentoring programmes, which include children and young people in care as part of their target group, or they may be specialised programmes targeted specifically at this group.

It is generally accepted that there is a dearth of research focusing specifically on the outcomes of formal mentoring programmes tailored to young people in care and leaving care (Spencer, Collins, Ward, & Smashnaya, 2010; Britner & Collins, 2018). Spencer et al. (2010) argue that the rapid growth in mentoring programmes for young people in care has occurred in the absence of clear empirical support for the effectiveness of these programmes. Johnson, Pryce, and Martinovich (2011) describe research on behavioural outcomes for foster youth in mentoring relationships as 'promising but limited' (p. 53). In this review, we focus on research evidence in relation to mentoring for children and young people in care that is undertaken as part of general mentoring programmes, specialised or intensive mentoring programmes and leaving care mentoring programmes.

General mentoring programmes: Much of the evidence regarding the benefits of youth mentoring for children in care is derived from studies of general youth mentoring programmes and focuses on these children and young people as a sub-set of a larger study. For example, one of the first studies to examine the outcomes of mentoring specifically for children and young people in foster care is a study by Rhodes, Haight, and Briggs (1999), which used data from the large scale flagship experimental study of the Big Brothers Big Sisters programme in the United States (Tierney, Grossman, & Resch,

1995). Rhodes et al. (1999) examined the effects of formal mentoring on the peer relationships of 90 young people in foster care aged 10 to 16 years. The baseline data showed that young people in foster care appeared to have more difficulty with close relationships and trust than did young people who were living with their parents. Tracked over 18 months, however, young people in foster care who had a mentor showed improvements in self-esteem and peer support over time compared to those without a mentor. Foster parents were more likely to report that their young person showed improved social skills and improved peer relationships as a result of the intervention. The authors suggest that mentors may help to support the young person in dealing with potential difficulties in peer relationships due to their experiences in foster care. This study also showed that foster parents were more likely than non-foster parents to seek a mentor for their child because the child was 'insecure and did not trust adults' (Rhodes et al., 1999, p. 197).

While not having a specific focus on children and young people in care, Herrera, Dubois, and Grossman (2013) explored the experiences and benefits of mentoring programmes for higher risk young people. The study assessed the effects of mentoring for 1,310 young people aged 8 to 15 years who were deemed to be 'high risk'. They found that youth mentoring programmes reached young people with varying 'risk profiles' and that these young people had relationships of similar strength and duration and derived similar benefits from programme participation. The key benefits found were reduced depressive symptoms, gains in social acceptance, academic attitude and results.

Somewhat in contrast to the findings of Herrera et al. (2013), research by Stelter, Kupersmidt, and Stump (2018) found that mentees in foster care had shorter matches and matches that were more likely to close prematurely than mentees who were not in foster care. Their study analysed information management databases from 216 Big Brothers Big Sisters agencies serving 641 youth in foster care and 70,067 youth not in care from across the United States in one-to-one, community-based (55.06%) and school- or site-based (44.94%) matches. They also found that youth in foster care were, on average, slightly older than youth who were not in foster care at the time they were matched with a mentor. The mentors with whom they were matched were more likely to be older and to have professional experience in a helping profession such as social work, mental health or education. While matches were shorter for foster care youth, however, the average match was still 12 months or more, which is in line with best practice. The authors surmise that the differing profile of mentors highlights that mentoring programmes are attuned to the need to ensure that young people in foster care are matched with experienced and mature mentors who will be equipped with the skills and dispositions to respond to their needs.

Intensive mentoring models specifically for children and young people in care: A number of studies have focused on enhanced or intensive approaches to mentoring for children in care, which have yielded positive results. For example, a study by Johnson and Pryce (2013) examined the benefits of therapeutic mentoring in helping to reduce trauma symptoms in foster youth. Therapeutic mentors are carefully selected, receive training in how best to respond to young people with traumatic experiences and receive ongoing supervision and training from clinicians. Mentors and mentees met for a fixed time every week and engage in shared activities. Outcomes were compared for mentored ($n = 106$) and non-mentored ($n = 156$) foster youth in relation to experience and symptoms of trauma. Results showed that mentored youth improved significantly in the reduction of trauma symptoms relative to non-mentored youth. The authors found that the frequency and duration of mentoring appeared to have a significant influence on whether or not the relationship led to positive outcomes.

Taussig and Culhane (2010) conducted a randomised controlled trial of a nine-month intensive mentoring and skills group intervention for children in foster care. The mentors participating in this study were all postgraduate students in social work or psychology and the programme included the delivery of a manualised curriculum that was specifically developed to address the needs of youth in foster care. They found improved mental health outcomes and quality of life for children in foster care who participated in the mentoring program compared to children who did not have a mentor.

Mentoring projects for young people leaving care: A number of studies have focused on mentoring for young people leaving care. Clayden and Stein (2005) conducted a study of a network of locally based mentoring projects for young people leaving care established by the Princes Trust and Camelot Foundation, in partnership with the National Children's Bureau in the United Kingdom. A total of 17 young people and 12 mentors were interviewed and 181 case files reviewed as part of the study. Clayden and Stein found that voluntary mentors were seen by young people to offer a different type of relationship to those provided by professionals or by family members. Mentors were seen to provide practical assistance, such as advice in relation to accommodation, education, employment and training as well as emotional support, including listening and helping with relationship problems. Young people valued the mentoring relationship for building confidence and improving their emotional well-being.

Clayden and Stein argue that that all young people take steps backwards and forwards when making the transition to adulthood and that young people in care are no different. Young people's needs and circumstances changed over the course of the relationship, so the mentor had to be responsive to these changing needs. The mentoring relationship was most successful where it was 'a flexible and dynamic process, working "with", not "on", young people' (p. 4). One young person, Clarice, who took part in the study, explained why she felt a mentor is needed for young people leaving care: mentored for three years:

> 'Cos when you leave care, you're in a flat, you're by yourself, you know. You need someone there to support you. Not everyone has family, not everyone has friends, but I think a mentor is essential.
> (quoted in Clayden and Stein 2005, p. 4)

In a US study, Osterling and Hines (2006) reported on an evaluation of the Advocates to Successful Transition to Independence programme, a mentoring programme designed to train mentors to assist older adolescent foster youth in acquiring skills and resources needed for successful transition out of foster care and into adulthood. Their findings suggested that the use of a mentoring programme for older adolescent foster youth may help to prevent negative outcomes as youth leave the foster care system and transition into adulthood.

> **Practice example: mentoring for young people leaving care**
>
> SAYes, based in Cape Town, South Africa, runs a range of mentoring programmes for young people leaving care. More than 15,000 young people are living in children's homes in South Africa, typically placed there by the courts due to issues including abuse, neglect and abandonment. According to SAYes, these young people can become marginalised from their communities and struggle to integrate into society when they leave care. Government support for young people in care in South Africa ends abruptly at the age of 18 and there is currently no transition support for care leavers.
>
> SAYes programmes are designed to prepare young people currently living in or recently exited from Child and Youth Care Centres (Children's Homes) for independent living. Each mentee meets with a trained mentor on a weekly basis for nine months and also attends monthly workshops to help to develop a transition plan for the young person. According to the 2016 annual report, the organisation supported 281 mentees between 2010 and 2016, with many mentees going on to experience careers in hospitality, retail and in the corporate world. Find out more at: http://sayesmentoring.org/about/

There are also examples of many education based mentoring programmes for young people leaving care. For example, Kirk and Day (2011) describe an initiative developed by Michigan State University to help young people leaving care to be successful in higher education. The programme included peer support, role modelling, mentoring and active learning sessions led by lecturers and students who were often foster care alumni themselves. Their study found that participants reported increases in knowledge and information about college life, funding and admissions procedures. Similarly, Brustera and Coccomaa (2013) describe a mentoring project using social work students as mentors and young people in foster care as mentees, with the aim of increasing the mentees' awareness of educational possibilities beyond high school graduation. These studies have shown that mentoring programmes can be valuable for young people ageing out of care.

4.5 Challenges and practice considerations in formal mentoring programmes for children in care

Efforts to replicate the benefits of natural mentoring relationships for young people in care through formal mentoring programmes can face a range of challenges. Because it is likely that young people in care have experienced disappointments and difficulties in their previous relationships, many have advised that there is a need to proceed very carefully when it comes to establishing a new relationship that may also end in disappointment and potentially pose a risk to the well-being of the young person (Courtney, 2009; Spencer et al., 2010; Collins & Ford, 2010):

> Introducing a failed or disappointing relationship in the life of any young person has the potential to be detrimental to his or her well-being, and this is likely to be especially true for foster youths who have already suffered significant disruptions in relationships with adults.
> (Spencer et al., 2010, p. 230)

Young people who have experienced abuse or maltreatment may experience attachment issues which can manifest as poor self-esteem, lack of trust in others and wariness in relationships (Spencer et al., 2010; Stelter et al., 2018). These experiences may lead to difficulties forming attachments with other adults, which may in turn prevent them from benefiting from mentoring relationships (Rhodes, 2005).

Furthermore, the capacity of the mentor to become a 'significant adult' in the life of the young person may be made more difficult by the transient and changing nature of young people's lives. Spencer et al. (2010) argue that the difficult circumstances faced by young people transitioning out of care may make it more difficult to form a stable relationship with a relative stranger. Clayden and Stein (2005) found that half of the relationships in their study of a leaving care project in the United Kingdom had some negative outcomes including a lack of engagement, missing appointments and unplanned endings – often linked to chaotic lives. In a fifth of these cases, the mentor withdrew and no longer met with and supported the young person. However, where young people had unplanned endings, some had achieved positive outcomes prior to that time. Herrera et al. (2013) reported that programme staff reported difficulties in accessing some young people due to frequent moves, homelessness and care placements. As noted earlier, Stelter et al. (2018) found that mentoring relationships for young people in care were shorter than the overall average for BBBS participants in the United States.

In addition, there is evidence that some young people do not feel comfortable accessing the support of a mentor through a formal programme. Young care leavers in the United Kingdom taking part in a qualitative study by Newton, Harris, Hubbard, and Craig (2017) expressed a preference for a long-term informal mentor rather than a formalised shorter-term relationship, the type offered through mentoring programmes. They suggest that, rather than provide the mentors, the mentoring organisation could facilitate the recruitment and training of non-kin existing 'natural mentors', whose support might continue to be available beyond the average length of a formal mentoring relationship. This model of youth initiated mentoring was discussed in Chapter 3.

According to Stelter et al. (2018) there is growing evidence supporting the potential of mentoring for being an effective intervention to address the needs of and promote positive outcomes of youth in foster care. However, there is a substantial gap in the literature regarding what intervention components contribute to the development of an enduring mentoring relationship and what practices aid programs in being most effective for this population of youth.

4.6 Conclusion

Following the focus on natural and youth initiated mentoring in Chapter 3, this chapter has provided an overview of research in relation to formal youth mentoring in general and youth mentoring for children in care specifically. The benefits and challenges of formal youth mentoring have been highlighted, some of which resonate with those associated with natural mentoring discussed in Chapter 3. Formal mentoring in the context of children in care has clear benefits given that children in care often do not have their own sustained and sustainable social support networks and can be dealing with issues that require a level of training and formal support from mentors to be able to give adequate support. Where programmes are in place for children in care, their evidenced success, notwithstanding the limits and challenges, suggests that there is potential to use this method of support for young people in care more extensively and as an integrated part of an overall support programme. We now move on to focus in further detail on formal mentoring for children in care, outlining the context and findings of a qualitative of study undertaken with young people in Ireland regarding their experiences of mentoring while in care. The study context and methodology are outlined in Chapter 5, while the findings are addressed in Chapters 6 and 7.

Summary points

- Studies of formal mentoring show that it a modestly effective intervention for youth at risk for a range of psychosocial and academic problems across four main areas: psychological and emotional well-being, social development, social behaviour and educational outcomes.

- Positive mentoring relationships usually involve a close and trusting relationship between individuals with similar interests who meet frequently.
- Mentor training, background and style impacts on the mentoring relationship.
- Focused mentoring programmes for children in care usually benefit the young person especially in relation to building confidence and improving his or her emotional well-being.
- Due to the complexity of the issues a young person in care may have experienced or may be experiencing, it must be acknowledged that mentoring can be more difficult to set up and mentors are likely to need more training and support.
- There remain gaps in the evidence to show what types of mentoring work best in different contexts and evidence is weak in some areas to show strong links between mentoring and positive outcomes for children and young people in care.

References

Albright, J. N., Hurd, N. M., & Hussain, S. B. (2017). Applying a social justice lens to youth mentoring: A review of the literature and recommendations for practice. *American Journal of Community Psychology*, 59(3–4), 363–381.

Allen, T. D., & Eby, L. T. (Eds.). (2011). *The Blackwell handbook of mentoring: A multiple perspectives approach*. Chichester, UK: John Wiley & Sons.

Aseltine, R. H., Dupre, M., & Lamlein, P. (2000). Mentoring as a drug prevention strategy: An evaluation of across ages. *Adolescent and Family Health*, 1(1), 11–20.

Barry, M. M., Clarke, A. M., Morreale, S. E., & Field, C. A. (2018). A review of the evidence on the effects of community-based programs on young people's social and emotional skills development. *Adolescent Research Review*, 3(1), 13–27.

Brady, B., & Curtin, C. (2012). Big Brothers Big Sisters comes to Ireland: A case study in policy transfer. *Children and Youth Services Review*, 34(8), 1433–1439.

Britner, P. A., & Collins, C. M. (2018). Permanent and formal connections. In E. Trejos-Castillo & N. Trevino-Schafer (Eds.), *Handbook of foster youth* (pp. 473–487). New York, NY: Routledge.

Brustera, B. E., & Coccomaa, P. (2013). Mentoring for educational success: Advancing foster care youth incorporating the core competencies. *Journal of Human Behaviour in the Social Environment*, 23(3), 388–399.

Busse, H., Campbell, R., & Kipping, R. (2018). Examining the wider context of formal youth mentoring programme development, delivery and maintenance: A qualitative study with mentoring managers and experts in the United Kingdom. *Children and Youth Services Review*, 95, 95–108.

Cavell, T. A., & Elledge, L. C. (2014). Mentoring and prevention science. In D. L. DuBois & M. J. Karcher (Eds.), *Handbook of youth mentoring* (pp. 29–43). Thousand Oaks, CA: Sage Publications.

Chapman, C. M., Deane, K. L., Harré, N., Courtney, M. G., & Moore, J. (2017). Engagement and mentor support as drivers of social development in the project K youth development program. *Journal of Youth and Adolescence, 46*(3), 644–655.

Clayden, J., & Stein, M. (2005). *Mentoring young people leaving care – 'Someone for me'*. York: The University of York and the Joseph Rowntree Foundation.

Collins, N. L., & Ford, M. B. (2010). Responding to the needs of others: The caregiving behavioral system in intimate relationships. *Journal of Social and Personal Relationships, 27*(2), 235–244.

Courtney, M. E. (2009). The difficult transition to adulthood for foster youth in the U. S: Implications for the state as corporate parent. *Society for Research in Child Development, 23* (2009), 3–19.

Crul, M. R. J., & Schneider, J. (2014). *MENTORING: What can support projects achieve that schools cannot?* Brussels: Migration Policy Institute Europe.

De Wit, D. J., DuBois, D., Erdem, G., Larose, S., & Lipman, E. L. (2016). The role of program-supported mentoring relationships in promoting youth mental health, behavioral and developmental outcomes. *Prevention Science, 17*(5), 646–657.

De Wit, D. J., DuBois, D., Erdem, G., Larose, S., Lipman, E. L., & Spencer, R. (2016). Mentoring relationship closures in Big Brothers Big Sisters community mentoring programs: Patterns and associated risk factors. *American Journal of Community Psychology, 57*(1–2), 60–72.

Deane, K. L., Harré, N., Moore, J., & Courtney, M. G. R. (2016). The impact of the project K youth development program on self-efficacy: A randomized controlled trial. *Journal of Youth and Adolescence*, 1–22.

Deutsch, N. L., & Spencer, R. (2009). Capturing the magic: Assessing the quality of youth mentoring relationships. *New Directions for Youth Development, 2009*(121), 47–70.

Dolan, P., Brady, B., O'Regan, C., Russell, D., Canavan, J., & Forkan, C. (2011). *Big Brothers Big Sisters (BBBS) of Ireland: Evaluation study*. Child and Family Research Centre, NUI Galway, and Foróige. Retrieved from https://aran.library.nuigalway.ie/bitstream/handle/10379/4498/BBBS_Report_3.pdf?sequence=1&isAllowed=y

DuBois, D. L., & Keller, T. E. (2017). Investigation of the integration of supports for youth thriving into a community-based mentoring program. *Child Development, 88*(5), 1480–1491.

DuBois, D. L., Holloway, B. E., Valentine, J. C., & Cooper, H. (2002). Effectiveness of mentoring programs for youth: A meta-analytic review. *American Journal of Community Psychology, 30*(2), 157–197.

DuBois, D. L., Portillo, N., Rhodes, J. E., Silverthorn, N., & Valentine, J. C. (2011). How effective are mentoring programs for youth? A systematic assessment of the evidence. *Psychological Science in the Public Interest, 12*(2), 57–91.

Durlak, J. A., & DuPre, E. P. (2008). Implementation matters: A review of research on the influence of implementation on program outcomes and the factors affecting implementation. *American Journal of Community Psychology, 41*(3–4), 327.

Erdem, G., DuBois, D. L., Larose, S., De Wit, D., & Lipman, E. L. (2016). Mentoring relationships, positive development, youth emotional and behavioral problems: Investigation of a mediational model. *Journal of Community Psychology, 44*(4), 464–483.

Gelis, J. F. (2015). How an intervention project contributes to social inclusion of adolescents and young people of foreign origin. *Children and Youth Services Review, 52*, 144–149.

Grossman, J. B., & Rhodes, J. E. (2002). The test of time: Predictors and effects of duration in youth mentoring relationships. *American Journal of Community Psychology, 30*(2), 199–219.

Grossman, J. B., & Tierney, J. P. (1998). Does mentoring work? An impact study of the Big Brothers Big Sisters program. *Evaluation Review, 22*, 403–426.

Herrera, C., DuBois, D. L., & Grossman, J. B. (2013). *The role of risk: Mentoring experiences and outcomes for youth with varying risk profiles, executive summary*. New York, NY: A Public/Private Ventures project distributed by MDRC.

Herrera, C., Grossman, J. B., Kauh, T. J., Feldman, A. F., & McMaken, J. (2007). *Making a difference in schools: The Big Brothers Big Sisters school-based mentoring impact study*. Philadelphia, PA: Public/Private Ventures.

Herrera, C., Grossman, J. B., Kauh, T. J., & McMaken, J. (2011). Mentoring in schools: An impact study of Big Brothers Big Sisters school-based mentoring. *Child Development, 82*(1), 346–361.

Holt, L. J., Bry, B. H., & Johnson, V. L. (2008). Enhancing school engagement in at-risk, urban minority adolescents through a school-based, adult mentoring intervention. *Child & Family Behavior Therapy, 30*(4), 297–318.

Johnson, S. B., & Pryce, J. M. (2013). Therapeutic mentoring: Reducing the impact of trauma for foster youth. *Child Welfare, 92*(3).

Johnson, S. B., Pryce, J. M., & Martinovich, Z. (2011). The role of therapeutic mentoring in enhancing outcomes for youth in foster care. *Child Welfare, 90*(5), 50–69.

Jolliffe, D., & Farrington, D. P. (2007). *A rapid evidence assessment of the impact of mentoring on re-offending: A summary*. London: Home Office.

Kaplan, S. J., Skolnik, L., & Turnbull, A. (2009). Enhancing the empowerment of youth in foster care: Supportive services. *Child Welfare, 88*(1), 133–161.

Karcher, M. J., & Herrera, C. (2007). School-based mentoring. *Youth Mentoring: Research in Action, 1*(6), 3–16.

Karcher, M. J., & Nakkula, M. J. (2010). Youth mentoring with a balanced focus, shared purpose, and collaborative interactions. *New Directions for Youth Development, 2010*(126), 13–32.

Keller, T. E., & Pryce, J. M. (2012). Different roles and different results: How activity orientations correspond to relationship quality and student outcomes in school-based mentoring. *The Journal of Primary Prevention, 33*(1), 47–64.

Kirk, R., & Day, A. (2011). Increasing college access for youth aging out of foster care: Evaluation of a summer camp program for foster youth transitioning from high school to college. *Children and Youth Services Review, 33*(7), 1173–1180.

Kupersmidt, J. B., Stump, K. N., Stelter, R. L., & Rhodes, J. E. (2017). Predictors of premature match closure in youth mentoring relationships. *American Journal of Community Psychology, 59*(1–2), 25–35.

Larsson, M., Pettersson, C., Skoog, T., & Erickson, C. (2016). Enabling relationship formation, development, and closure in a one-year female mentoring program at a non-governmental organization: A mixed-method study. *BMC Public Health, 16*(1), 179.

Liang, B., Spencer, R., West, J., & Rappaport, N. (2013). Expanding the reach of youth mentoring: Partnering with youth for personal growth and social change. *Journal of Adolescence, 36*(2), 257–267.

Lipman, E. L., De Wit, D., DuBois, D. L., Larose, S., & Erdem, G. (2018). Youth with chronic health problems: How do they fare in main-stream mentoring programs? *BMC Public Health, 18*(1), 102–131.

MacCallum, J., Beltman, S., Coffey, A., & Cooper, T. (2014). *Youth mentoring relationships: Understanding how to prevent breakdown*, Mentoring Worx – Academic Research, Australian Government, Dept. of Education/Government of Western Australia, Dept. of Local Government and Communities.

Matz, A. K. (2013). Commentary: Do youth mentoring programs work? A review of the empirical literature. *Journal of Juvenile Justice, 3*(2), 83–101.

Meyerson, D. A. (2013). *Mentoring youth with emotional and behavioral problems: A meta-analytic review* (Unpublished doctoral dissertation), DePaul University, Chicago, IL.

Miller, A. (2007). Best practices for formal youth mentoring. In T. D. Allen & L. T. Eby (Eds.), *The Blackwell handbook of youth mentoring: A multiple perspectives approach* (pp. 307–324). Malden, MA: Blackwell Publishing.

Morrow, K. V., & Styles, M. B. (1995). *Building relationships with youth in program settings: A study of Big Brothers/Big Sisters*. Philadelphia, PA: Public/Private Ventures.

Newton, J. A., Harris, T. O., Hubbard, K., & Craig, T. K. J. (2017). Mentoring during the transition from care to prevent depression: care leavers' perspectives. *Practice, 29*(5), 317–330.

Osterling, K. L., & Hines, A. M. (2006). Mentoring adolescent foster youth: Promoting resilience during developmental transitions. *Child & Family Social Work, 11*(3), 242–253.

Philip, K., & Hendry, L. B. (2000). Making sense of mentoring or mentoring making sense? Reflections on the mentoring process by adult mentors with young people. *Journal of Community & Applied Social Psychology, 10*(3), 211–223.

Philip, K., & Spratt, J. (2007). *A synthesis of published research on mentoring and befriending*. Manchester: The Mentoring and Befriending Foundation.

Prieto-Flores, Ò., & Gelis, J. F. (2018). What type of impact could social mentoring programs have? An exploration of the existing assessments and a proposal of an analytical framework. *Pedagogia Social, 31,* 149–162.

Raposa, E. B., Rhodes, J. E., & Herrera, C. (2016). The impact of youth risk on mentoring relationship quality: Do mentor characteristics matter? *American Journal of Community Psychology, 57*(3–4), 320–329.

Raposa, E. B., Rhodes, J., Stams, G. J., Card, N., Burton, S., Schwartz, S., . . . Hussain, S. (2019, March). The effects of youth mentoring programs: A meta-analysis of outcome studies. *Journal of Youth and Adolescence, 48*(3), 423–443.

Rhodes, J. (2019a). Two logical fallacies that distract the field of mentoring. *Chronicle of Evidence Based Mentoring*. Retrieved from www.evidencebasedmentoring.org/two-logical-fallacies-that-distract-the-field-of-mentoring/

Rhodes, J. (2019b, March 7). Five key takeaways from a comprehensive new meta-analysis of youth mentoring. *Chronicle of Evidence Based Mentoring*. Retrieved from www.evidencebasedmentoring.org/five-key-takeaways-from-a-comprehensive-new-meta-analysis-of-youth-mentoring/

Rhodes, J. E. (2005). A model of youth mentoring. In D. L. DuBois & M. J. Karcher (Eds.), *Handbook of youth mentoring* (pp. 30–43). Thousand Oaks, CA: Sage Publications.

Rhodes, J. E., Haight, W. L., & Briggs, E. C. (1999). The influence of mentoring on the peer relationships of foster youth in relative and nonrelative care. *Journal of Research on Adolescence, 9*(2), 185–201.

Rodríguez-Planas, N. (2012). Mentoring, educational services, and incentives to learn: What do we know about them? *Evaluation and Program Planning, 35*(4), 481–490.

Simões, F., & Alarcão, M. (2014). Promoting well-being in school-based mentoring through the satisfaction of basic psychological needs: Does it really count? *Journal of Happiness Studies, 15*(2), 407–424.

Spencer, R. (2007). "It's not what I expected" A qualitative study of youth mentoring relationship failures. *Journal of Adolescent Research, 22*(4), 331–354.

Spencer, R., Basualdo-Delmonico, A., Walsh, J., & Drew, A. L. (2017). Breaking up is hard to do: A qualitative interview study of how and why youth mentoring relationships end. *Youth & Society, 49*(4), 438–460.

Spencer, R., Collins, M. E., Ward, R., & Smashnaya, S. (2010). Mentoring for young people leaving foster care: Promise and potential pitfalls. *Social Work, 55*(3), 225–234.

Spencer, R., Gowdy, G., Drew, A. L., & Rhodes, J. E. (2019). "Who knows me the best and can encourage me the most?": Matching and early relationship development in youth-initiated mentoring relationships with system-involved youth. *Journal of Adolescent Research, 34*(1), 3–29.

Stelter, R. L., Kupersmidt, J. B., & Stump, K. N. (2018). Supporting mentoring relationships of youth in foster care: Do program practices predict match length? *American Journal of Community Psychology, 61*(3–4), 398–410.

Taussig, H. N., & Culhane, S. E. (2010). Impact of a mentoring and skills program on mental health outcomes for maltreated children in foster care. *Archives of Pediatric and Adolescent Medicine, 164*(8), 739–746.

Tierney, J. P., Grossman, J. B., & Resch, N. L. (1995). *Making a difference: An impact study of Big Brothers/Big Sisters*. Philadelphia, PA: Public/Private Ventures, and United States of America.

Tolan, P. H., Henry, D. B., Schoeny, M. S., Lovegrove, P., & Nichols, E. (2014). Mentoring programs to affect delinquency and associated outcomes of youth at risk: A comprehensive meta-analytic review. *Journal of Experimental Criminology, 10*(2), 179–206.

Walker, G. (2005). Youth mentoring and public policy. In D. L. DuBois & M. J. Karcher (Eds.), *Handbook of youth mentoring* (pp. 510–524). Thousand Oaks, CA: Sage Publications.

Williams, C. A. (2011). Mentoring and social skills training: Ensuring better outcomes for youth in foster care. *Child Welfare, 90*(1), 59–74.

5 Introducing the current study

5.1 Introduction

Thus far in this volume, we have reviewed theory and literature in relation to natural mentoring and formal mentoring in general and specifically for children in care. We now move on to present the findings of a research study which was undertaken to inform this book. The research involved in-depth qualitative interviews with 13 young people with care experience who had taken part in a youth mentoring programme in Ireland. The study aims to understand young people's subjective experiences of the mentoring relationship in the context of their overall lives. This chapter contextualises the study, providing an overview of the policy and legislation in relation to child welfare in Ireland. It also describes the Foróige Big Brothers Big Sisters youth mentoring programme from which research participants were drawn. The rationale for the study is outlined, followed by the research methodology employed in the study, including design, ethical considerations and analysis. The chapter concludes with a profile of research participants and summary messages.

5.2 Child welfare in Ireland

Policy in relation to children and young people in Ireland has undergone radical change over the past few decades. Prior to the early 1990s, laws providing protection and welfare to children and young people had remained mostly unchanged since 1908. Since the enactment of the Child Care Act (1991), there has been a significant growth in legislation and policy related to children and families, increased investment of resources in the child care system and the expansion of personnel and services in a variety of domains. Ireland has moved towards a rights based approach for children through its ratification of the UN Convention on the Rights of the Child (UNCRC) in 1992, and in 2012, the people of Ireland voted to strengthen the rights of children in the Irish constitution. Other significant developments include the development of the first national strategy for children and young people (Our Children, Their Lives: National Children's Strategy, 2000) followed by the Better Outcomes, Brighter Futures: The National Policy Framework for

Children and Young People, 2014–2020. A Children's Ombudsman Office was created in 2004 and separate minister and Department for Children and Youth Affairs has been in existence in Ireland since 2011, showing an increasing visibility and focus of Irish social policy in matters relating to children and the family.

Another significant development has been the Task Force on the Child and Family Support Agency which reported in 2012 and led to the development of an independent child and family agency in Ireland for the first time in 2014. Tusla, as the Irish national Child and Family Agency has been named, was established in 2014 as part of a major reform of child protection, early intervention and family support services. Tusla is responsible for the provision of child protection and welfare, family support and education welfare services in Ireland. This includes social work services, foster care, residential care and special care. Tusla employs more than 4,000 staff across Ireland. Tusla offers a range of services to families who are experiencing difficulties, which include social work, family support workers, youth workers, family resource centres, support groups and counselling services (Tusla, n.d.). Some of the core services like child protection and some family support are provided directly from the statutory service. Many other services are provided on behalf of Tusla by voluntary organisations, such as Barnardos, Foróige, Extern and the Youth Advocate Programme. Ireland has historically relied heavily on voluntary/third sector organisations to deliver key services, and such partnerships continue to play a central role in the service provision (Dukelow & Considine, 2017).

As part of this ongoing process of reform, significant advances in the development of alternative care provision have occurred in Ireland in recent decades. Traditionally reliant mostly in institutional care up to the 1970s, family based care is now the preferred option in Ireland (Burns & McGregor, 2019). Of the 6,190 children in care in Ireland in November 2018, the vast majority were cared for in foster placements, either by relative foster parents (27%) or by approved foster families (65%) (www.tusla.ie/data-figures/). Gilligan (2019) notes that, along with Australia, Ireland now has one of the highest rates of family placements in child welfare systems globally. Tusla may receive children into care through a voluntary agreement (voluntary care) with parents or by way of a court order. Recent figures indicate that 32% of children admitted to care during 2017 were admitted under a voluntary care arrangement (www.tusla.ie/data-figures/).

A key issue for child welfare provision in Ireland at present is the difficulty of recruitment and retention of social workers within Tusla. Tusla social workers have an average of 30 caseloads per social worker, while the international average is closer to 15 (Power, 2017; Burns & McGregor, 2019). These resourcing issues have implications for the capacity of Tusla to respond adequately to child welfare needs. As of November 2018, there were 24,891 cases relating to child protection and welfare concerns, of which 19.7% of cases had yet to be allocated a social worker. Figures also indicate that 95% of children in care had an allocated social worker, while 92% had a written care plan (www.tusla.ie/data-figures/). Another major issue in the current child welfare system is court delays and processes and the complications for children in care caused by this as evidenced in the Child Care Law Reporting Project that has reported on court processes for children in the child protection system, including those in care (Coulter, 2015, 2018).

The legacy of widespread abuse of children in institutional care in Ireland such as that captured in the *Report of the Commission to Inquire into Child Abuse* (Ryan Report, 2009) continues to resonate deeply. In addition to needing to take responsibility and account for the harm done to survivors of the time, this disclosure of systematic failures to take account of children's subjective needs and interests or their well-being has emphasised in the present the importance of direct relational work with children, the challenging of dominant power relations, the promotion of partnership and the establishment of an ethos of children's rights. There is an eagerness in the present system to learn new approaches, improve direct work with children, enhance participation work with children and young people and be innovative in working with the child as central (Burns & McGregor, 2019). A greater emphasis on working more closely with children and young people and enhancing participation, for example through the use of Signs of Safety in child protection and the use of the child centred 'meitheal' family support model, are opening up opportunities for social work to expand its focus on relationship based and preventative practices (Rodriguez, Cassidy, & Devaney, 2018; Tierney, Kennan, Forkan, Brady, & Jackson, 2018).

While youth mentoring has not explicitly been a core part of social work practice up to now, both approaches share common aims and purposes relating to meeting the best interests of young people. The possibility for youth mentoring to emerge as an area of child welfare practice in this context is notable. Imagine, for example, what it would have been like had each child in care, in the past, had one 'reliable adult' assigned to them over their childhoods and into young adulthood to support him or her in his or her development, dreams and aspirations, well-being and future planning for adult life. A core aim of this book is to consider how we might maximise this potential and give guidance to support its realisation in practice.

5.3 Setting for the study: the Foróige Big Brothers Big Sisters programme

The research for this study was conducted with young people in care who have been matched with an adult mentor under the Foróige Big Brother Big Sister programme. Foróige is a large Irish youth organisation which aims to involve young people consciously and actively in their own development and in the development of society. The core philosophy of the organisation is to encourage young people to be part of shaping the world around them while developing their talents, skills and abilities. Foróige works with over 50,000 young people aged 10–18 annually through volunteer-led clubs, staff-led youth projects and youth cafés throughout Ireland. The organisation also runs a range of programmes through its network of clubs and projects, including Youth Entrepreneurship, Youth Citizenship, Youth Leadership, Relationships and Sexuality and Politics. In addition to its universal youth work, Foróige (n.d.) works with vulnerable young people who require additional support through a range of targeted services.

Over two decades ago, Foróige identified a gap in its range of services – that of a one-to-one volunteer-led support service in the community for young people experiencing a range of difficulties. The internationally recognised Big Brothers Big Sisters programme was chosen to meet the identified need (Brady & Curtin, 2012). Foróige became the host organisation for BBBS in Ireland in 2001 and became an affiliated member of Big Brothers Big Sisters International.[1] Unlike the US model which generally sees mentoring offered as a stand-alone programme, the Irish BBBS programme is integrated into the range of services on offer in local Foróige youth projects. Many of the Foróige youth workers are also trained as BBBS caseworkers which means that they can identify young people who would benefit from mentoring through youth work services and can also link young people taking part in mentoring into wider youth work services or programmes as appropriate (Brady & Curtin, 2012).

The Foróige Big Brothers Big Sisters programme matches an adult volunteer to a young person (aged between 10 and 18) of the same gender. The aim of the programme is to facilitate the development of a caring and supportive friendship that will reinforce the positive development of the young person. The target group for the programme is young people who would benefit from additional support in their lives, including those identified as being at high risk, such as young people in residential and foster care, young people involved in the criminal justice system and separated youth seeking asylum in Ireland (McGregor, Lynch, & Brady, 2017). The programme, therefore, is not specifically targeted at young people in care but some participants are or have been in care. Young people can be referred to the programme by professionals such as social workers, youth workers or teachers, while family or self-referral is also possible. In general, the programme does not have strict criteria regarding what types of risk are suitable or unsuitable – it is guided by a consideration of whether or not the young person would benefit from the programme and if he or she is suitable for matching with a volunteer (Dolan et al., 2011).

In this programme, the relationship is known as 'the match', the mentor is referred to as the Big Brother or Sister and the mentee is known as Little Brother or Sister. Participation in the programme is voluntary for both the young person and mentor. The mentor and mentee meet once a week, for one to two hours, and the initial commitment is for one year. The friendship between the mentor and mentee is considered the most important aspect of the intervention. During the first six months of the match, the focus is on building a solid relationship, developed through shared and mutually enjoyable leisure activities such as sport, music, cooking, board games, computers, fishing or going to football matches. It is envisaged that a close connection will develop between the adult and young person, which will become the foundation for the young persons to learn from their mentors and be open to accepting support, advice and direction from them in the months to follow. Once a close relationship has been established, goals aimed at addressing the needs of the young person may be agreed by all parties. For example, goals might be related to learning a new skill or hobby, school attendance, academic performance or community involvement (McGregor et al., 2017). The matches are managed by project officers who are employed by Foróige.

The Irish Big Brothers Big Sisters programme was evaluated using a randomised control trial methodology with a sample of 164 young people (Dolan et al., 2011). Standardised survey measures were used to assess outcomes for young people aged 10–14 years at four time points over a two-year period for intervention and control groups. The outcomes assessed related to four dimensions – emotional and mental well-being, education, risk and problem behaviour and relationships and social support. The RCT results show that the mentoring intervention was effective in relation to emotional well-being and social support, with statistically significant findings for the intervention *versus* control group analysis at Wave 4. The study found that the programme was particularly beneficial for young people who did not live with both parents. The research also found the Irish BBBS programme showed strong adherence to best practice standards in youth mentoring (Dolan et al., 2011).

Big Brothers Big Sisters International affiliations have also been evaluated in a number of other countries. For example, in a large scale study with participants in the BBBS Canada programme, De Wit, DuBois, Erdem, Larose, and Lipman (2016) examined the relationship between youth mentoring status and behavioural, developmental and emotional outcomes for 859 youths aged 6–17 years. The findings revealed that mentored youths, especially those in mentoring relationships lasting 12 or more months, reported significantly fewer behavioural problems and fewer symptoms of depression and social anxiety than did non-mentored youths. They also reported stronger coping skills and emotional support from parents. A cost-benefit analysis of the Big Brothers Big Sisters Melbourne programme undertaken by Moodie and Fisher (2009) concluded that the programme represents 'excellent value for money' when the potential cost savings of preventing adult criminality are taken into account.

5.4 Rationale for the current research study

While the voices of children and young people were historically marginalised in research (France, 2004), children have increasingly been the focus of research studies over recent decades. As a result of influences such as the

UNCRC, the children's rights movement and the new sociology of childhood, research with children has evolved from seeing children as 'static unthinking objects' to respecting children as 'dynamic reasoning agents' (Alderson, 2004, p. 110; Fleming, 2010) and as 'competent and reliable witnesses to their own lives' (France, 2004, p. 177). While involving children and young people in research is now commonplace, Kennan and Dolan (2017) caution there must be a well-reasoned and transparent ethical justification for their inclusion in research in order to avoid over-researching children's experiences or asking them to give up their time in return for little or no value. They highlight that researchers must fulfil their ethical duty to protect children and young people from harm, 'while respecting their autonomy as social actors and independent rights holders to participate in research of relevance to their lives'(2017, p. 309). The need for a strong rationale for research is particularly salient when the research involves children and young people deemed to be vulnerable.

Before undertaking this research, therefore, it was important to reflect on the justification for doing it. Young people in care are potentially a very vulnerable group. In many cases, these young people will enter into the care of the state as a result of neglect, abuse and family breakdown and may be suffering the negative effects of these events. Furthermore, living in care can, in some cases, be a stressful and challenging experience for young people. However, the need to ensure that the voices of children in care are heard has been well documented in Ireland and internationally (Jackson, Brady, Forkan, Tierney, & Kennan, 2018). A number of Irish reports spanning decades, from the Kennedy Report in 1969 to the more recent Ryan Report (2009), highlighted the serious failings of the state to protect children as a consequence of not listening to them (Martin, Forde, Dunn Galvin, O'Connell, & O' Gráda, 2015). Still in the present day, many children and young people in care can often feel that they don't have a say in decisions that affect them (McEvoy & Smith, 2011; McGregor et al., 2017). Research can play an important role in facilitating young people in care to articulate their views regarding their experiences of services and programmes and to have their voices heard and responded to (Jackson et al., 2018; Moran, McGregor, & Devaney, 2017; Shannon, 2016; Stein, Pinkerton, & Kelleher, 2000). In order to establish the value or benefits of mentoring for young people in care, therefore, research is needed that allows young people to articulate the meaning and value of mentoring in the context of their lives. While we saw in Chapters 3 and 4 that research has been conducted on mentoring for children in care, much of this research was undertaken in North America and was quantitative in nature. There is a dearth of qualitative studies focusing on young people in care's perspectives on mentoring in other cultural contexts. Moreover, much mentoring research is focused on outcomes for young people who are currently taking part or have recently finished a mentoring programme, leading to calls for more studies focusing on the longer term effects of youth mentoring relationships (Prieto-Flores &

Gelis, 2018). It was felt that there was a strong justification, therefore, to gain an in-depth insight into young people in care's experiences of mentoring. By including both current participants and previous participants of the programme, it was hoped that insights would be gleaned regarding both the short-term and longer-term impacts of mentoring from the perspectives of young people in care.

5.5 Study overview

Detailed one-to-one narrative style interviews were conducted with 13 young people who are currently or were previously participants in the BBBS youth mentoring programme while in care. The core aim of the study was to explore how young people describe and interpret the significance of their relationship with their mentor and its impact on their overall life and care experience.

Qualitative methods are described by Ritchie, Lewis, Nicholls, and Ormston (2013) as naturalistic, interpretative approaches used to examine particular phenomena. A qualitative narrative approach was chosen for the study because it offers the potential to elicit a deep understanding of the meanings that people place on actions, events, and relationships that they have experienced (Castleberry & Nolan, 2018). It has been argued that qualitative research, which seeks to understand and represent lived experiences and perceptions, is the ideal approach for understanding child and youth experiences (Schelbe et al., 2015).

Narrative research is a qualitative research approach that 'privileges the voices of participants and dissemination of lived experience through thick description and storytelling' (Mcnamara, 2013, p. 138). Reissman (2008) argues that people naturally tell stories to make sense of their experiences. The strength of a narrative methodology, therefore, is that it allows people to tell stories about their lives in a relatively organic way, using their own words (Hill & Dallos, 2011). It has also been argued that narrative-based methods align with the decolonization of research, positioning participants as authorities on their own lives and allowing them to direct the tone and focus of their narratives (Liebenberg, Wood, & Wall, 2018). In recent years, there has been an increasing use of narrative approaches in research with children (Moran, Reilly, & Brady, in press). As well as facilitating children and young people to share their understandings of key events using their own words, it has been argued that narrative style research can also help them to make sense of the world and their place in it (Engel, 2006).

Research advisory group

Children's participation has been defined as 'the process by which children and young people have active involvement and real influence in decision-making on matters affecting their lives, both directly and indirectly' (DCYA,

2015, p. 20). The movement towards children's participation in decision making also extends to participation in decision making about research. In order to ensure that the study was conducted in a way that was respectful of and attentive to the experiences of young people in care, it was considered important to enable the participation of young people with relevant experience in the research design (Leeson, 2007).

At the study design stage, a Research Advisory Group was established, composed of three young people aged 18 to 24 years who had previously been in care and/or participated in a mentoring programme. The role of this group was to provide feedback regarding various aspects of the study design and implementation. The group provided feedback on matters such as ethical considerations, the design and wording of information sheets and consent forms and the approach used in interviews.

Sampling and recruitment

In January 2018, Foróige identified all young people in care who were taking part in the BBBS programme at that point in time or who had previously taken part. It was established that at that juncture that 15 young people who had aged out of care and an additional 31 young people currently in care would be eligible to take part. In order to ensure adherence to their data protection policy, Foróige acted as gatekeepers for the study recruitment. BBBS project officers were asked to contact potential participants and to speak to them about the study and ask if they would be interested in taking part. This was felt to be appropriate as the Foróige staff member would generally have formed a relationship with the young person as part of the BBBS intervention. If they indicated a willingness to take part, the BBBS officer then sent information sheets and consent forms to the young person (and their designated guardian for those aged under 18 years) and answered any questions they had if required. The researchers contact details were also made available should the young persons or their guardians have any questions. The young persons were given a minimum of one week to decide if they wished to take part. All potential participants were made aware of their right to not take part and their right to change their mind about participation at any time during the study. They were also informed that deciding not to participate would not affect any of the services provided to them by Foróige. A small number of young people were not approached because of particular vulnerabilities they were experiencing at the time of the study.

Information sheets and consent forms were distributed, outlining the aim of the study, the role of the young person in the research and the potential risks and benefits associated with participation. The procedures for gaining consent were different for the cohort aged under 18 and those aged over 18 years.

- *Young people under 18:* Potential participants were contacted by Foróige in the first instance, informed about the study and asked for

young person and caregiver consent. Foróige contacted the appropriate caregiver to seek consent (e.g. parent, foster parent, social worker). If the young person and his/her guardian gave consent, their contact details were then passed on to the researcher, who proceeded to arrange an interview with the young person.
- *Young people over 18 years:* Potential participants were contacted by Foróige, informed about the study and asked for the young person's consent. If the young person gave consent, his or her contact details were passed on to the researcher, who then proceeded to arrange an interview with the young person.

A total of 19 young people agreed to take part in the study, of whom six subsequently changed their minds and opted not to be interviewed. Therefore, 13 young people took part in interviews; a profile of the sample is provided later in the chapter. The sample does not claim to be representative of the experiences of all young people in care who took part in Big Brothers Big Sisters. It is possible that people with more positive experiences were more likely to self-select for participation.

Ethical considerations

There were a number of ethical considerations associated with the study. Ethical approval was granted by the NUI, Galway Research Ethics Committee. Given that the study participants were young people in care, there was a risk of emotional upset for the participants during or after the interview as a result of speaking about sensitive personal issues and experiences. Participants were advised of this possibility in the study information sheets and verbally by Foróige staff and were also told that they could stop the interview at any time. A distressed persons' protocol was developed to guide the researcher in supporting research participants, should they become upset. Participants were also given the option of bringing a friend to the interview if they wished, though none did so. Support was also available from the Foróige BBBS Project Officers should it be required.

Another key ethical consideration for the study was the risk of disclosure of abuse – present or previous – which had occurred in the young person's life. All participants were informed in the written information sheets and verbally at the start of the interview that in the case that they disclosed such information, or from speaking to them that the researcher had reason to believe that a child protection issue existed, she was obliged to follow the Children First 2011 Guidelines and to pass the information on to Tusla Child and Family Agency. No disclosures of concern were made.

Anonymity or confidentiality were also of critical importance due to the personal details provided in young people's narratives and the possibility of identification. Efforts were made to ensure that no identifying information was revealed in the resulting report. Minor changes were made to aspects of

86 Introducing the current study

the young people's narratives that would make it possible to identify them. It was also decided that a cross-sectional thematic approach would be used to present findings, rather than a case study approach which would leave participants more open to identification.

Interviews

Interviews were conducted in a narrative style, where the emphasis was placed on open-ended questions that allowed the young persons to tell their stories. The aim of the interviews was to allow the young persons to recount in their own words how they came to take part in the mentoring programme and their experiences of it. Following advice given by the Research Advisory Group, participants were informed that the main focus of the interview was on their experience of having a mentor and that they could share 'as much or as little' as they wanted about their own life experience outside of the mentoring relationship. To begin, young people were asked to tell their story of how they came to have a mentor in their lives and following this, several topics were probed, including: if they felt they had changed as a result of the mentoring relationship, if they trusted their mentor, if they could recall particular moments that were important to them, how their mentor was different from other people in their social network and if they felt that mentoring is a good idea for children in care.

All interviews were conducted face-to-face by the lead author and took place in a variety of locations throughout Ireland, including Foróige offices or other community centres (9), the young person's foster home (2), a café (1) and the researcher's office (1). The researcher aimed to ensure that the interview location was accessible and familiar to the participant and allowed for the interview to be conducted in a manner that protected the confidentiality of the participant. All participants were sent a thank you card and small token of appreciation after the interviews.

Data analysis

All interviews were transcribed in full and data was analysed using a process of Thematic Analysis (TA). The purpose of TA is to identify patterns of meaning across a dataset that provide an answer to the research question being addressed. Patterns are identified through a rigorous process of data familiarisation, data coding and theme development and revision. For the purposes of this study, the process of analysis was inductive or data driven, whereby no specific coding frame or pre-conceptions were used to shape the findings. However, it is acknowledged that the researchers were not working 'in an epistemological vacuum' (Braun & Clark, 2006, p. 84) and are likely to have been influenced by prior reading and research on this topic.

The data was analysed using the six-phase process outlined by Braun and Clark (2006):

1 **Familiarisation with the data**: During this phase, all transcripts were read in full on numerous occasions to allow the researchers to become familiar with its content.
2 **Coding**: A large number of labels (or codes) were assigned to parts of the texts in order to identify similarities and differences in the data. Examples of codes assigned at this stage included 'like family', 'how mentor is different to social worker', 'confidence', and so on.
3 **Searching for themes**: All codes were examined and were grouped together to identify significant broader patterns of meaning or potential themes. According to Braun and Clark (2006, p. 82), 'a theme captures something important about the data in relation to the research question, and represents some level of patterned response or meaning within the data set'. At this stage, some broad themes were identified including the benefits that accrued from the relationship – emotional well-being, social connectedness, education and identity development. The data relevant to each theme was grouped under that theme, which helped to assess its viability.
4 **Reviewing themes**: The entire dataset was re-read at this stage in order to ascertain whether the emerging themes were sufficiently accurate and comprehensive. This resulted in some themes being discarded or merged with others.
5 **Defining and naming themes**: During this phase, the focus was on further refinement of the scope and focus of each theme. Final names for each theme were decided.
6 **Writing up**: The final phase of the analysis process involved writing up the analysis, using quotes to illustrate the points made and locating the findings in terms of the wider literature.

The findings were grouped into two broad categories. The first category relates to the benefits or outcomes that young people attributed to the mentoring relationship. There are four themes under this heading; social and emotional well-being, educational engagement and progression, social capital and civic engagement,= and identity development. These findings are outlined in Chapter 6. The second category, which is elaborated on in Chapter 7, encompasses young people's views on the characteristics of their mentors and of the mentoring relationship and their perspectives on how it differed to their relationships with social workers, family and friends.

5.6 Profile of the research participants

Of the 13 young people who took part in the study, ten were female and three were male and ranged in age from 13 to 24. As shown in Table 5.1,

88 Introducing the current study

Table 5.1 Profile of research participants in terms of age, sex and match status

Name	Age	Sex	Match status	Length of match
Grace	14	Female	Currently matched	1–2 years
Lily	14	Female	Currently matched	3–4 years
Maeve	14	Female	Previously matched	1–2 years
Sophie	14	Female	Currently matched	1–2 years
Chloe	15	Female	Currently matched	2–3 years
Roisín	15	Female	Currently matched	1–2 years
Edel	17	Female	Currently matched	5 years plus
Sean	18	Male	Previously matched	5 years plus
Robin	18	Female	Previously matched	4–5 years
Mary	19	Female	Previously matched	2–3 years
James	21	Male	Previously matched	4–5 years
Rachel	21	Female	Previously matched	5 years plus
Sarah	24	Female	Previously matched	5 years plus

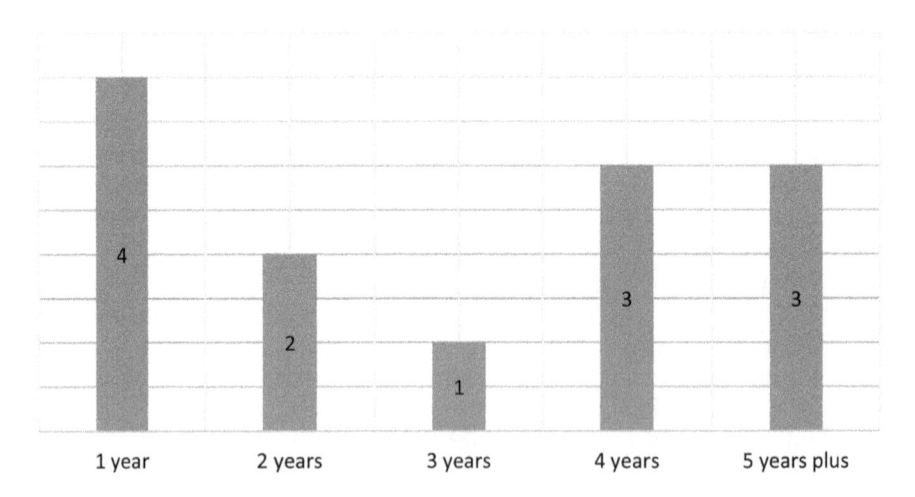

Figure 5.1 Number of years matched
Source: Authors' research

all research participants had been 'matched' with their mentor for at least one year, with a range of match length times across the sample. Four participants were matched for five years or more (see Figure 5.1).

5.7 Conclusion

The aim of this chapter was to provide a context and background for the research findings presented in Chapters 6 and 7. While there are many ongoing issues and problems with the Irish child welfare system, considerable progress has been made over the past number of decades in the development of a more caring and child centred child care system. The Foróige

Big Brother Big Sister Mentoring programme operates within the voluntary sector but works with a range of young people, including those who have engagement with child welfare services, including children in care. This research study was designed and conducted to explore the perspectives of young people in care regarding their experiences of mentoring and to better understand the mechanisms through which mentoring can support children in care. What follows in Chapters 6 and 7 is a detailed outline of the findings from this study.

Summary messages

- The child welfare and protection system in Ireland has evolved significantly to allow greater scope for supportive, preventative and relationship based practice.
- Research participants are currently or had had been matched with mentors as part of the Foróige Big Brothers Big Sisters youth mentoring programme while in care. All research participants had been 'matched' with their mentor for at least one year, while four participants were matched for five years or more.
- The design of the research study was supported by a Research Advisory Group of young people with experience of care and/or mentoring and paid particular attention to ethical considerations such as risk of emotional upset, disclosures and availability of support post-interview.
- Narrative style interviews were conducted with 13 young people aged between 14 and 24 years, with the emphasis was placed on open-ended questions that allowed the young person to tell their story.
- Data was analysed using a process of thematic analysis.

Note

1 Big Brothers Big Sisters International was founded in 1998 with the aim of promoting and supporting the development of Big Brother Big Sister mentoring programmes operating independently in various countries.

References

Alderson, P. (2004). Ethics. In S. Fraser, V. Lewis, S. Ding, M. Kellett, & C. Robinson (Eds.), *Doing research with children and young people* (pp. 97–112). London: Sage.

Brady, B., & Curtin, C. (2012). Big Brothers Big Sisters comes to Ireland: A case study in policy transfer. *Children and Youth Services Review*, 34(8), 1433–1439.

Braun, V., & Clarke, V. (2006). Using thematic analysis in psychology. *Qualitative Research in Psychology*, 3(2), 77–101.

Burns, K., & McGregor, C. (2019). Child protection and welfare systems in Ireland: Continuities and discontinuities of the present. In *National Systems of Child Protection* (pp. 115–138). Berlin: Springer.

Castleberry, A., & Nolen, A. (2018). Thematic analysis of qualitative research data: Is it as easy as it sounds? *Currents in Pharmacy Teaching and Learning*, 10(6), 807–815.

Coulter, C. (2015). *Final report: Child care law reporting project*. Retrieved from www.childlawproject.ie/interim-reports/

Coulter, C. (2018). *An examination of lengthy, contested and complex child protection cases in the district court*. Retrieved from www.childlawproject.ie/interim-reports/

De Wit, D. J., DuBois, D., Erdem, G., Larose, S., & Lipman, E. L. (2016). The role of program-supported mentoring relationships in promoting youth mental health, behavioral and developmental outcomes. *Prevention Science*, 17(5), 646–657.

Department of Children and Youth Affairs (DCYA). (2015). *National strategy on children and young people's participation in decision-making*. Dublin: Government Publications.

Dolan, P., Brady, B., O'Regan, C., Russell, D., Canavan, J., & Forkan, C. (2011). *Big Brothers Big Sisters (BBBS) of Ireland: Evaluation study*. Galway: Child and Family Research Centre, NUI Galway, and Foróige.

Dukelow, F., & Considine, M. (2017). *Irish social policy: A critical introduction*. Bristol: Policy Press.

Engel, S. (2006). Narrative analysis of children's experience. In S. Greene & D. Hogan (Eds.), *Researching children's experiences* (pp. 199–216). London: Sage.

Fleming, J. (2010). Young people's involvement in research: Still a long way to go? *Qualitative Social Work*, 10, 207–223.

Foroige. (n.d.). *About Foroige*. Retrieved from www.foroige.ie/

France, A. (2004). Young people. In S. Fraser, V. Lewis, S. Ding, M. Kellett, & C. Robinson (Eds.), *Doing research with children and young people* (pp. 175–190). London: Sage.

Gilligan, R. (2019). The family foster care system in Ireland – Advances and challenges. *Children and Youth Services Review*, 100, 221–228.

Hill, K., & Dallos, R. (2011). Young people's stories of self – Harm: A narrative study. *Clinical Child Psychology and Psychiatry*, 17(3), 459–475.

Jackson, R., Brady, B., Forkan, C., Tierney, E., & Kennan, D. (2018). *Collective participation for children in care: A formative evaluation of the Tusla/EPIC foster care action groups*. Galway: UNESCO Child and Family Research Centre, National University of Ireland, Galway.

Kennan, D., & Dolan, P. (2017). Justifying children and young people's involvement in social research: Assessing harm and benefit. *Irish Journal of Sociology*, 25(3), 297–314.

Leeson, C. (2007). My life in care: Experiences of non-participation in decision-making processes. *Child & Family Social Work*, 12, 268–277.

Liebenberg, L., Wood, M., & Wall, D. (2018). Participatory action research with indigenous youth and their communities. In R. Iphofen & M. Tolich (Eds.), *Handbook of qualitative research ethics* (pp. 339–353). London: Sage.

Martin, S., Forde, C., Dunn Galvin, A., O'Connell, A., & O' Gráda, A. (2015). *An examination of children and young people's views on the impact of their participation in decision-making*. Dublin: Government Publications.

McEvoy, O., & Smith, M. (2011). *Listen to our voices! hearing children and young people living in the care of the state*. Dublin: Government Publications.

McGregor, C., Lynch, M., & Brady, B. (2017). Youth mentoring as a form of support for children and young people at risk: Insights from research and practice. In P. Dolan & N. Frost (Eds.), *The Routledge handbook of global child welfare* (pp. 345–357). London: Routledge.

Mcnamara, P. (2013). Rights-based narrative research with children and young people conducted over time1,2. *Qualitative Social Work*, *12*(2), 135–152.

Moodie, M. L., & Fisher, J. (2009). Are youth mentoring programmes good value for money? An evaluation of the Big Brothers Big Sisters Melbourne program. *BMC Public Health*, *9*, 1–9.

Moran, L., McGregor, C., & Devaney, C. (2017). *Outcomes for permanence and stability for children in long-term care*. Galway: UNESCO Child and Family Research Centre.

Moran, L., Reilly, K., & Brady, B. (Eds). (in press). *Narrating childhoods across contexts: Knowledge, environment, and relationships*. London: Palgrave Macmillan.

Power, J. (2017, June 3). Over 400 children in State care are without a social worker. *The Irish Times*. Retrieved from www.irishtimes.com/news/social-affairs/over-400-children-in-state-care-are-without-a-social-worker-1.3107226

Prieto-Flores, Ò., & Gelis, J. F. (2018). What type of impact could social mentoring programs have? An exploration of the existing assessments and a proposal of an analytical framework. *Pedagogia Social*, *31*, 149–162.

Reissmann, C. (2008). *Narrative methods for the human sciences*. London: Sage.

Ritchie, J., Lewis, J., Nicholls, C. M., & Ormston, R. (Eds.). (2013). *Qualitative research practice: A guide for social science students and researchers*. London: Sage.

Rodriguez, L., Cassidy, A., & Devaney, C. (2018). *Meitheal and child and family support networks final report: Tusla's programme for prevention, partnership and family support*. Galway: UNESCO Child and Family Research Centre.

Ryan Report. (2009). *Report of the commission to inquire into child abuse*. Dublin: Stationery Office.

Schelbe, L., Chanmugam, A., Moses, T., Saltzburg, S., Williams, L. R., & Letendre, J. (2015). Youth participation in qualitative research: Challenges and possibilities. *Qualitative Social Work*, *14*(4), 504–521.

Shannon, G. (2016). *Ninth report of the special rapporteur on child protection: A report submitted to the Oireachtas*. Dublin: Department of Child and Youth Affairs.

Stein, M., Pinkerton, J., & Kelleher, P. (2000). Young people leaving care in England, Northern Ireland, and Ireland. *European Journal of Social Work*, *3*(3), 235–246.

Tierney, E., Kennan, D., Forkan, C., Brady, B., & Jackson, R. (2018). *Tusla's programme for prevention, partnership and family support: Children's participation work package final report*. Galway: UNESCO Child and Family Research Centre.

6 Young people's perspectives on the benefits of mentoring

6.1 Introduction

Having introduced the study context and methodology in Chapter 5, we now move on to outline the research findings. In this chapter, we focus in detail on young people's accounts of how their relationships with their mentors was meaningful to them. The findings are presented under four thematic areas which emerged from an analysis of narratives of young people as the benefits they associated with the relationship. The first theme is that of *social and emotional well-being*. Young people spoke of social and emotional issues they experienced in their lives, including social isolation, loneliness and feelings of stress and anger and of the ways in which the relationship with the mentor helped them to cope with these issues. The support provided was pivotal in terms of enabling young people to deal more effectively with pressures faced in many areas of their lives, including in their family relationships and within the education system. Second, the theme of challenges and difficulties faced in relation to *educational engagement and progression* was a prominent one across the young people's narratives. Young people spoke of how their care experience had impacted negatively on their school experience and of how the support of their mentors helped them to overcome challenges and to achieve a more positive engagement with the education system. Third, young people described how they had developed new social networks and connections, with some taking up leadership and volunteering roles as a result of involvement in the BBBS programme, which is discussed under the heading of *social capital and civic engagement*. Fourth, the theme of *transition and identity* was prominent in the narratives of some of the older participants in particular, whereby mentors were seen to offer support to young people in making the transition to early adulthood and in developing a coherent sense of identity.

6.2 Social and emotional well-being

It is common for children to experience challenges to their social and emotional well-being during adolescence. Young people in care can face

Table 6.1 Summary of themes arising in relation to social and emotional well-being

Social and emotional issues experienced	How mentoring helped	How young person feels they have benefited
Loneliness / social isolation	Someone to talk to/meet every week	Feel happier
Lack of close attachments – family	Sharing mutually enjoyable activities	Feel less stressed
Not having someone to talk to	Having fun – a break from normal life	Can put things into perspective
Feeling stressed and/or angry	Someone to talk about 'little' and 'big' things	Better understand own emotions and behaviour
Lack of confidence/ difficulties mixing in groups	Learning new ways to deal with emotions	Enhanced capacity to manage anger
Low self-esteem	Engaging in new social contexts	More confident
	Having someone who cares about you	Find it easier to talk to people
	'Having to learn to talk' to mentor and others	

additional pressures, particularly where they have experienced multiple transitions (Winter, 2012) and may have to deal with a range of emotions around separation, loss, attachment, trauma and bereavement (Healey & Fisher, 2011). In this section, the ways in which youth mentoring relationships were seen to contribute to enhancing social and emotional well-being among research participants is reviewed, including providing a social outlet, listening and emotional support, understanding and dealing with emotions and increased confidence. The key findings in relation to social and emotional wel-being are summarised in Table 6.1.

Providing a social outlet

A number of participants said that looking back to the start of their mentoring relationship, they were actually quite socially isolated, lonely or bored. Meeting up with their mentor was described as providing a welcome break from boredom, an opportunity to get out of the house or to get off the streets.

> I was sitting at home pretty much the whole time doing nothing other than at the weekends I'd meet my friend but that was only for like one day for a couple of hours. But meeting up with Stephen then during the week was great to get out and get a bit of exercise and social time as well; I wasn't going to crack up.
>
> (Sean, 18)

> I feel like it's, like if we're getting in so much trouble and stuff it just gets you off the streets just keeps your mind of everything like, you're doing something with someone, than you're just not like . . . on the streets.
>
> (Maeve, 14)

Many of the research participants described the activities they engaged in with their mentors as enjoyable and relaxed. Some liked to do sports, such as squash, swimming or rowing. For example, Sean (18) and his mentor Stephen tried squash on their first meeting and continued to do it every week for seven years. Others preferred to hang out, go for walks, go shopping or go to cafés. Whether active or passive, the activities were often described as 'fun'.

> He was like, what do you want to do and I was like, sure I might as well try squash. Gave it a go and we're playing it since . . . I taught him every rule and every different way to hit the ball; I showed him everything about it. He loves it now.
>
> (Sean, 18)

> We went out for lots of spins, brought her dog out for walks and stuff . . . went shopping, was so much fun.
>
> (Mary, 19)

Listening and emotional support

Some young people spoke of how they appreciated having 'someone there for me' present in their lives on a consistent basis whom they could talk to and feel listened to. For them, the knowledge that they could chat to someone about their feelings was a source of comfort. Many of the research participants said that they talked to their mentors about day-to-day stuff that was happening in their lives, such as school, hobbies, friends and boyfriends or girlfriends. Participants spoke of feeling a lack of judgement and a sense of acceptance from their mentor.

> Because you just talk to somebody and get to know somebody and just spend time with them.
>
> (Chloe, 15)

> She was always there for me and if ever I needed to talk to anyone she was always there for me to talk to and she's nice.
>
> (Grace, 14)

> Any advice I wanted I could get from her like. About you know? If there was a boy I liked or whatever like.
>
> (Mary, 19)

96 *Young people's perspectives on mentoring*

For some young people the match provided an opportunity to also talk about their feelings about family and their experiences in care. They said they found it valuable to have someone outside of family, foster parents, siblings or friends to talk to about deeply personal issues. For example, Edel spoke of how she valued the support from her mentor when life was very difficult for her.

> Even when my foster placements were really bad breaking down like when I was like really bad with like depression or anything I had Joan you know? Say at different times and like they were like, they just make you feel so much better about yourself.
>
> (Edel, 17)

Many of the research participants said that talking to their mentor helped them to deal with anger and stress in their daily lives. For example, Robin said that her worries and anxieties are lessened by talking to her mentor.

> If you're having a bad day you know. . . . Just lifts all the stuff and it just makes you think. . . . It wasn't that bad you know. . . . It's not that bad talking to someone . . . just nice to know that you can talk to someone.
>
> (Sophie, 14)

Similarly, Roisín described how she contacts her mentor, Fiona, during the week if something is bothering her. She gave the example of receiving support from Fiona when she was getting into trouble at school; rather than getting angry she said that she sorted it out with Fiona's help.

> If I ever need her sometimes during the week, I have her phone number so I text if there was something that I needed to talk about like, instead of getting angry about something or whatever. I'd go straight to Fiona about it. She was just like staying really calm about everything when I was ranting about it so she listens, she listens to everything that I have to say.
>
> (Roisín, 15)

Lily lives in family foster care with her aunt and uncle, who also have three small boys under the age of eight. She said their house is 'just crazy'. Lily's mother is currently undergoing drug treatment and she has been in care twice. She described her relationship with her dad as 'complicated'. Lily values her match as somewhere that is just for her; she uses it to talk about her feelings about her family situation, which in turn has helped her to deal with what is going on in her life.

> I kind of use my match as someone just to talk to about everything that is going on at home and stuff. . . . It's just that I feel like if I talk to someone outside of like, not the real world but like outside of that

> kind of world, that kind of space. . . . It's like my own thing that I have to myself. I don't think I could handle everything that's going on right now, like being in care and having all the problems and all. . . . I haven't noticed anything in particular how it's changed me but in my head, in my feelings if I didn't have Olivia I don't know who I would be able to talk to. . . . Olivia comes and takes me out so I'm getting away from all the stress and it's made me not that stressed.
>
> (Lily, 14)

Lily said that she had tried counselling but it didn't work for her because she doesn't feel comfortable talking about her feelings in a more formal setting. She described the match as more like a friendship, which makes it easier for her to talk, saying 'It's kind of easy-going and you go coffee places and you do baking and cooking'.

James described how now, in his early twenties he can still call on his mentor, Tony, for a chat if he is feeling stressed.

> I meet up with him now; if I ever want to talk to him like, if I'm stressing about work or something; if I have a stressful day I'll ask him to meet up to have a coffee or something and chat.
>
> (James, 21)

Understanding and dealing with emotions

As well as listening, many of the research participants said that their mentors help them to understand their emotions, to put them in context and to identify ways that they can react differently to situations. For example, Sophie described how her mentor helped her to understand why she felt nervous and to see that lots of other people felt that way too, while Lily's mentor helped her to develop more productive ways of coping with her emotions.

> I think talking to her about why I was nervous or you know? Like what made me nervous and like her saying that everything is going to be fine and you know? All people are nervous all the time and it's like, it's not the end of the world.
>
> (Sophie, 14)

> I have this teacher I don't like and . . . I just exploded one day in class. . . . Once you push my button like I just explode. But like I seen Olivia that week and she just calmed me like, calmed me down and just was like it's not like a big deal. . . . She was like instead of doing that, talk like how I'm talking now. Calm and collected. And I took that onboard. I'm trying that new technique out, being calm and collected but it's like not getting, I'm not right there yet but I'm trying to work on it.
>
> (Lily, 14)

Similarly, Grace (14) and Rachel (21) spoke about their tendencies to get angry and said that the strategies their mentors had given them for dealing with anger had helped.

GRACE: She just like gave me tips and ideas and how to behave and if I get angry or something, not to lash out.
INTERVIEWER: And if someone else had given you those tips like, if you'd seen them on the telly or whatever do you think it would have made a difference?
GRACE: I wouldn't have listened to them, no.

> In first year, I got expelled (from school). I used to have a lot of anger issues. . . . And yes, she taught me to control my anger. So now instead of getting cheeky and getting violent or verbally aggressive what I do is I just go to the gym or I leave the room or I just go take ten minutes and have a cup of tea and think about it or write it down on paper or and then address it when I'm more calm.
> (Rachel, 21)

Similarly, Sarah spoke of how Ciara's calm and positive response to difficult situations helped her to view situations that arose in her residential care setting in a more positive light. She said that she herself learned to view situations in this way.

> If I would have an issue in the house with somebody like 'oh he's a bit strange' or 'she's a bit strange' and then I'll say it to Ciara you know? She wasn't like; she would try as much as she can to just be positive about it you know? Forget about the negativity and just be positive you know? And so she was just always a positive person.
> (Sarah, 24)

Building self-confidence and sociability

A theme that emerged strongly across all the narratives is increased confidence and sociability. Many of the young people interviewed spoke about how their confidence had improved through meeting with their mentor. Research participants spoke of how they are now more sociable and better able to talk to people since taking part in BBBS. For example, James said that he was very anxious when meeting people but that Tony helped him to overcome this by gently introducing him to social settings. For James, developing this confidence has made a huge difference in his life as he is no longer held back from doing what he wants by fear.

> He slowly, without me knowing, kind of gave me confidence by taking me out to these places. Like in the cinema there's people around and I'm very bad with crowds and that but like he wouldn't; if I didn't like

something he would take me away from it like. Like I think things like that and then eventually taking me into Foróige groups (youth clubs) then; just get me into bigger like interacting with people more.

(James, 21)

A key issue for Sarah in her teenage years was the fact that she spoke English with a strong accent. Her relationship with Ciara provided a safe space where she could practice and improve her English. This helped Sarah to realise that it was an obstacle she could overcome, which built her confidence in herself and her right to engage in society. Similarly, Sophie feels that she is less shy and is better able to speak up in class. Having to engage with her mentor and make conversation on a weekly basis, in addition to being exposed to group events where she had to mix with other matches helped her to overcome this shyness.

> I was a lot more shy because I just didn't really like talking to people that I didn't know and I only really talked to a few kids in my school at the time. . . . But as I did the Big Brother Big Sister programme it like gained me a lot of confidence and I'm not as shy or I don't speak as quiet in class or anything like that, if I'm asked a question like I wouldn't be speaking into the desk or into my hands or anything like I would before and yes, it's helped me to get a lot of confidence which I'm glad about.
>
> (Sophie, 14)

In reflecting on the difference mentoring has made in his life, Sean also emphasised the development of his social skills, which has helped him in other aspects of his life and will continue to do so.

> Before I met Stephen I was very socially awkward like; I wouldn't really talk to anybody much but now I'd just go up to anybody and talk to them you know . . . I'd say it boosted my confidence more with like going to work and getting a job and having a decent life and improving my social skills.
>
> (Sean, 18)

For Sean, seeing his mentor, Stephen, who is an entrepreneur, talking to people on the phone as part of his work helped him to realise that talking to people was not that difficult. He also sees how this skill will be important to him in his future career.

> When he's with me sometimes he has to be working as well; he's supposed to be working at home but when he's meeting me he just still works and he's talking about all the people he'd be talking to and ringing them and everything and they'd be ringing him. He'd be sending emails and texts, all sorts. . . . Talking to people all the time and sure why not; it's not that big of a deal. . . . Especially now when I'm going to be working, like I need to be able to talk to people, clients.
>
> (Sean, 18)

Robin (18) said that before she took part in BBBS, she would not have to make an effort in conversations and 'was like agreeing with everyone' but when meeting up with her mentor, 'like we both had conversations so we both had to talk. . . . You had to; you couldn't be just there like yes'. As a result of this, Robin feels that she is better at 'like talking out and expressing my feelings towards things and not buckling things up'. Robin said that she had recently taken part in a public speaking event at school and 'I had confidence to go up and talk out' whereas before she 'wouldn't have been able to'. She feels that having a mentor is particularly valuable for children in care because 'when you're in care you're kind of, you're sticking to yourself . . . because a lot has gone on in your life before you went into care and then it's easier to talk to someone you didn't know who doesn't know anything about it'.

'Like family'

For some of the research participants, the emotional support provided by the mentoring relationship was deeply profound. Rachel and Sarah in particular developed a very deep relationship with their mentors and spoke of them as being 'authentic' and 'like family', describing how their mentor was there for them in good times and bad and at times such as Christmas which were often very difficult for them. Like the participants in a study by Schofield, Larsson, and Ward (2017, p. 789), their narratives reflect 'ways in which our shared cultural meanings for family are drawn on to capture the emotional feelings of being cared about and cared for'.

For example, Sarah (24) recounted how she had come to Ireland from Uganda when she was 12 with her parents and two siblings. A year after arriving, the family experienced issues and she and her siblings were placed in care. They lived in a variety of residential homes. Around this time, Sarah was matched with Ciara as part of the BBBS programme. Almost 12 years after their initial match, Sarah and Ciara are still regularly in touch. Sarah spoke about the difficulties of adjusting to life in a new country, her changed family situation and dealing with frequent placement moves in the care system. In this context, Sarah valued Ciara as being a consistent presence in the midst of change, someone she could rely on.

> If you don't have a family foundation . . . it's like having that person there that truly cares about you. . . . I remember one time at Christmas we were in a home and then she came first in the morning with her husband with Christmas stuff. . . . She didn't have to do that, showing up in that house on Christmas morning, like, those kind of memories will always you know? Stand by me. Just authenticity, it has like . . . really even shaped me as a person.
>
> (Sarah, 24)

Similarly, Rachel spoke of how she was taken into care when she was 12 but 'hated the idea of being in care'. Over the course of her teenage years, she experienced a great deal of change and turbulence but drew great comfort from the consistent presence of her mentor, Eve, and the wider BBBS staff team in her life. Like Sarah, it is over a decade since she first engaged with the BBBS programme and she still sees Eve as 'my sister'.

> Over the years I had four social workers and six foster houses, so the only consistent person throughout the whole process was Eve. . . . I still introduce her as my sister to everybody, she's practically family. I go to hers at Christmas and everything. . . . She's just become my sister as such.
>
> (Rachel, 21)

6.3 Educational engagement and progression

International research has found that large numbers of children in care leave school before completing secondary education and are less likely to pursue further or higher education (Daly & Gilligan, 2010). The theme of education came up consistently across the interviews. Many young people referred to their experiences of education being affected by the personal stress they had experienced. There were many examples given of how having the support of their mentor was instrumental in supporting them to relieve stress, approach situations differently and, as a result, have a more positive relationship with school.

Some research participants spoke of their mentor supporting them to have a better insight into their own behaviour and its consequences, particularly in a school context. For example, James said that he was always in conflict with teachers in school but that Tony helped him to see and understand his own role in creating the conflict. Once he had come to this realisation, he 'backed off' and became less of 'a messer' at school. As a result, James said that he started to enjoy school a lot more and had better relationships with teachers.

> I complained to him about, 'I don't get why teachers are against me all the time' but I was the one against them and he explained that to me but not in the way that I felt like he was having a go at me or anything. But he explained it; maybe you're the one, maybe you are talking out of turn and maybe the teachers just don't like that; just explaining things to me so I'd get it and realise it.
>
> (James, 21)

When asked if she had changed in any way as a result of taking part in BBBS, Roisín highlighted her approach to school and hobbies as the main change in her life. She described how she had been absent from school for long periods, which she attributed to feelings of anger. Roisín spoke of how talking to her mentor, Fiona, helped her to reduce her anger and feel less stressed.

> Like in third year now I used to never go to school. . . . Like I missed over a hundred days in third year. I used to never go to school and it was like the first time, it was like the only time I'd ever missed days in school. I just did not want to go to school. I did not want to do anything. I dropped out of dance and gymnastics and horse riding, I dropped out of everything. . . . And then when I started talking to Fiona [mentor], I was kind of more relaxed because I was always very very angry, like I don't know why I was angry, like the smallest thing would trigger me. And but yes when I started talking to Fiona it was kind of making everything more relaxed, it was taking the pressure off me that I was talking to people, because I would never talk to my [foster] Mom, but like it was just getting a lot of stuff out when I was talking to Fiona, so that made everything much easier and like I think now I'm back to going into school all the time and everything is grand and it's because I'm not holding in anything. Because I can talk to Fiona about everything.
> (Roisín, 15)

International research has found that educational attainment among children in care can be negatively impacted by frequent placement and school changes, increased rates of exclusions and absenteeism and low expectations of their ability among professionals and carers (Brady Gilligan, & Nic Fhlannchadha, 2019). These themes were articulated by Rachel, who said that school was always difficult for her because she had missed a lot of primary school and was 'always behind'.

> When I was 12 my school, when I went into care my school filed a report to say that I had the reading ability of a 9-year-old. So I was really behind since day one because I never really went to primary school. So I was really behind and I was always behind but it was expected, well why can't you do this and why do we have to get you grinds in this? Why can't you just do it yourself and then I stopped asking for help.
> (Rachel, 21)

As a result of her experiences, Rachel was frustrated and angry and eventually decided to drop out of school at age 15 after being expelled. She recounted how, at the time, she experienced a great deal of anger from her foster family and everyone 'shouting the face off me'. Her decision to go back to school came about as a result of working through the pros and cons of her decision with her mentor, Eve.

> Eve just put me in the car and we went for a spin, she made a pros and a cons list of the good ideas to leave school and the bad ideas and

obviously the bad list outdid the good . . . and she convinced me to go back.

(Rachel, 21)

Ultimately, Rachel decided to go to third level and received considerable support from Eve and the BBBS project officers with grinds and homework support, which she believes was instrumental in helping her to succeed in her Junior and Leaving Certificates. Rachel is now in her final year of college and plans to undertake a master's degree. She said that there is no way she would have considered going to third level without the encouragement and support of Eve and the BBBS staff because nobody else in her social network was encouraging her to go to college.

> In my foster homes a lot of them, they didn't, they weren't used to we'll say having people who wanted to go on to college so it was never encouraged. My family have always encouraged me to leave education by 16 because I have like a Traveller background as well, so it's culture to leave at 16.
>
> (Rachel, 21)

Like Rachel, Sarah also welcomed the advice and guidance of her mentor, Ciara, on the education system and the pathways she could take. This was particularly valued given that she and her family were not familiar with the Irish education system and because she was unsure of what direction she wanted to take.

> I did my Junior Cert and I did my Leaving Cert and like so she told me about her college experience but I still didn't know what I really wanted to do but having somebody that was once young like me and had to go through the education system, because she said she didn't know what she wanted to do either but eventually she got into, you know what I mean. . . . So she did inspire me that you don't have to know exactly what you want to do, it's just about making those choices that will lead you to a better future . . . build a foundation for yourself.
>
> (Sarah, 24)

Similarly, Edel referred to her mentor Joan's willingness to help her out with her schoolwork and projects in any way she could. There is a sense from Edel's narrative of shared enjoyment and excitement found in doing these things together.

> Like my Home Ec. project for my Junior Cert she was so helpful . . . and writing up CVs so I could get my first job. She was the one who was doing it with me and everything like. My Agricultural Science project

Table 6.2 Summary of themes arising in relation to educational engagement and progression.

Educational issues experienced	How the mentoring relationship helped	How the young people feel they have benefited as a result of mentoring
Behavioural problems at school	Emotional support	Less conflict at school
Falling behind at school academically	Helped to understand own behaviour / approach situations differently	Doing better at exams
Withdrawal from school/hobbies		Return to education
Being expelled from school/deciding to leave school	Hands on approach – grinds, college applications, grants	Progressing to Leaving Cert and college
No family member to help with college/career paths	Encouraging/acting as a sounding board for college/career paths	Career plans
Family/culture don't value education	Supporting a change in mindset about education	

now for my Leaving Cert, she is bringing me down to her uncle's farm and everything . . . and she loves it as well. She's very 'oh yes, we'll get this done for you now'.

(Edel, 17)

The findings in relation to educational engagement and progression are summarised in Table 6.2.

6.4 Social capital and civic engagement

The concept of social capital highlights that social connections and trust between people are beneficial to individuals and to society (Field, 2008; Putnam, 2000). Social capital is important to adolescent well-being by virtue of broadening networks and providing opportunities for interaction and resources with others, often through local groups and activities (Ferguson, 2006). Bonding social capital refers to ties that are often close, durable and strong on emotional support, while bridging social capital is characterised by weak ties with people who are not close but which may be beneficial in terms of their personal or career progression (Putnam, 2000). Many of the research participants spoke of developing bonding and bridging social capital through their mentoring relationships.

A number of participants described how they had broadened their social networks through taking part in social events organised by the BBBS programme. Sean referred to a trip to an adventure centre in the west of Ireland for matches from all over the country. He said he was initially reluctant to go, thinking 'I'm not going to like this at all' but that he got there he had a great time and met lots of new people. As a result he 'made two new friends; I talk to them a good bit now'. Edel also spoke of how she had developed social connections around the country as a consequence of taking part in the programme.

> You meet people and you have these friendships and these connections then for life, like I know someone in almost every county now because of Big Brother Big Sister.
>
> (Edel, 17)

Edel gave a very powerful description of what it is like not to have a close family around you at times of celebration. She believes that the bonding relationships she has developed through the Big Brothers Big Sisters programme will be the ones that she will draw on for support at those times in her life.

> There is often times say when I'm in foster care I think where am I going to go now? Like I think births, marriages like you know? Christmas, like where would I be going for Christmas dinner you know when I'm older if I don't have a close relationship with my family? And I remember like I could call these people at four o clock in the morning and they'd be there and they would be listening to you and they're all like no no no you're always welcome you know?
>
> (Edel, 17)

Having moved to Ireland from Uganda when she was 12 and subsequently going into care, Sarah greatly appreciated being introduced to a new social network by her mentor, Ciara, including Ciara's family, friends, and work connections. As well as being a volunteer Big Sister, Ciara worked as a youth worker so she connected Sarah to summer camps and youth groups, through which she made friends and became 'more established' in Ireland.

> If she wasn't there I probably wouldn't have gotten so many opportunities that I've gotten. . . . So there's so many doors that has opened for me, so many opportunities, so many people I've met that if I hadn't known Ciara I wouldn't have met them you know? It was really nice, it was just an opportunity that people around me weren't getting you know? And like that exposure has really helped me in so many ways that I can now be in a room full of other people that it wouldn't really bother me and I could interact with them and still have a good laugh.
>
> (Sarah, 24)

The concept of civic engagement is closely related to that of social capital and has been defined as 'individual or collective actions in which people participate to improve the well-being of communities or society in general' (Innovations in Civic Participation, 2010, p. vi). A number of participants said that, as a result of their experience with BBBS, they are currently volunteering or would like to get more involved with youth work when they are older. Rachel said that she is now a peer support mentor in her third level college. She volunteered for it to 'give back' because she had benefited so much from BBBS and feels she understands how it works in terms of supporting autonomous decision making.

> The only reason I do it (mentoring) is because Big Brother Big Sister used to do that with me. So I do it for them [students] now. It's kind of a give back process. . . . I'm only facilitating their learning, I don't give them the answers I just kind of push them which is kind of a lot like what Big Brother Big Sister does. It's like a jigsaw, they give you all the pieces and they urge you to put it together.
> (Rachel, 21)

The view was also articulated by some that, as a result of their experiences with the programme, they have a heightened awareness of how meaningful it can be for people going through challenging times to experience kindness and empathy. For example, Sarah spoke of how she is more attuned to her capacity to be a support to others because her mentor, Ciara, was such as support to her and her family.

> So even when I see other people that are not as fortunate as I am I try my best, ok, is there anything that I can do? You know? Maybe just buy them lunch. Or maybe just I can help you for an hour. You know? So it's like she was planting seeds in me but not bad seeds, seeds that you know? That would be of service to other people because she was as much of service to me as to my siblings as well you know?
> (Sarah, 24)

Edel has taken up leadership roles at national level within Foróige and outside the organisation, experiences which have fuelled her determination to pursue a career in youth work. She spoke of the many opportunities she has been given to develop her leadership skills, including training programmes, representing Foróige at an EU event in Brussels, acting as MC for a local awards night and being elected to a youth participation group at a high level within the organisation. In addition to her mentor who supports her with all these endeavours, Edel said she has been influenced positively by a range of inspirational youth workers, volunteers and managers she has met in the course of her involvement with the organisation and jokes that she has told the Foróige CEO that she has her eye on his job.

It has been acknowledged in the mentoring literature that older youth may benefit from the development of weak ties or bridging social capital with non-family members that can link them to education, training or employment opportunities (Van Dam et al., 2018; Raposa, Erickson, Hagler, & Rhodes, 2018). Rachel spoke of securing work experience through a relative

Table 6.3 Summary of themes arising in relation to social capital and civic engagement

Social issues experienced	How the mentoring relationship helped	How the young people feel they have benefited as a result of mentoring
Limited support network New cultural context Lack of social capital to secure work experience	Introduced young person to new social networks Linked to opportunities for leadership and volunteering Connected to employment opportunities	Made new friends and broadened social network More empathetic and aware of their capacity to make a difference to others Taken on new roles Giving back to society Clear plan for career in youth work Increased confidence

of one of the BBBS Project Officers, work experience which was critical to her securing a good work placement for her degree programme.

> I still had to go through interviews and stuff, he wasn't just hiring me because she said so as such and I still followed all the rules like anybody else and I still made mistakes that I got pulled on. . . . Then that got me my part-time job and it got me my work placement because I had done an internship.
>
> (Rachel, 21)

The findings in relation to social capital and civic engagement are summarised in Table 6.3.

6.5 Transition and identity

For young people in care, the process of leaving care can be difficult and challenging as they may not have the resources and supports that most young people take for granted. Mike Stein's early research describes different approaches to transitions and three different groups of young people: the 'moving on group', the 'survivors group' and the 'victims group'. Outcomes are better generally for young people when they have continuity and support from their foster families or other reliable adult supports (Christiansen, Havnen, Havik, & Andersen, 2013). While the research participants were not specifically asked about their transitions to adulthood, themes relating to transition and the type of future they wished for themselves came up frequently in the narratives.

Of the seven study participants aged 17 or older, most had been matched for at least four to five years and there was a sense from five young people that their relationship with their mentor was still important to them. Rachel, Sarah, James, Edel and Sean spoke of their mentors in the present tense and indicated that the mentor continued to be a positive influence in their lives. For two participants, Robin (18) and Mary (19) in this age cohort, the mentoring relationship was something they referred to as being in the past and which they had valued at the time but that they had now moved on. Both Robin and Mary said that they did not have an ongoing relationship with their mentors, apart from following each other on social media or the occasional text message. As highlighted earlier in this chapter, Robin felt she had become much more confident as a result of taking part in the programme. She gave the impression that she was 'moving on' confidently into a new phase of her life, enjoyed good support from her foster family and felt that the mentoring relationship had reached a natural conclusion. Mary spoke affectionately of her mentoring relationship, recalling many happy memories from the time she was matched. She feels that it benefited her to know that 'there's more people out there like me'. However, Mary referred to struggles she has since experienced with grief and loss and feels that when you are in care, you are 'stuck'. She did not see any enduring benefits for herself from the mentoring relationship and there were no indications from her narrative that the relationship had influenced her future plans.

> It's great in the moment but once it's done it's done you know?
> (Mary, 19)

The remaining five participants referred to ways in which their relationship with their mentor supported them in the transition to adulthood. Some of the influence with regard to positive transitions (e.g. education, social connections) has already been addressed in this chapter. The impact of the mentoring relationship was arguably greater for Rachel (21) and Sarah (24) who didn't have family relationships or other close attachments that they could depend on. James (21), Edel (17) and Sean (18) had good or reasonably good relationships with foster parents but gave insights into the ways in which their mentors also influenced their pathways. All five could be described as 'moving on' in that they were engaged in education, had a sense of purpose and a positive outlook for the future. In this section, we focus on how mentors influenced the young people's perspectives on the type of adult that young people wanted to be.

Identity development is a key developmental task during adolescence. Erickson (1968) suggests that adolescent identity achievement occurs after a period of exploration or 'moratorium'. As noted earlier in this book, one of the most challenging things about being in care can be the fact that for most children, it means taking on a dual or multiple identity as a member of their birth family and also of one or more foster families or placements (Moran, McGregor, & Devaney, 2017). For children in care, the process of identity development includes addressing a range of questions about their families and childhood experiences and about the type of person they want to be in the future. It may also involve dealing with stigma in relation to their family background and being in care (Rogers, 2017). Drawing on theorists such as Cooley (1902), Mead(1934) and Erickson (1968), who have argued that people's sense of self is influenced by the attitudes, behaviours and traits of people they wish to emulate, Rhodes (2005) posits that the mentoring process may influence the young person's conception of his or her current and future identity.

The narratives of these five participants suggest that they drew on the support of their mentors to encourage them with issues relating to identity, exploring who they are and who they want to be as a person. Like the participants in Schofield et al's study (2017), these discussions helped them to accept mixed feelings about their birth family and to gain confidence in themselves and their potential. In terms of their future life course, the young people were conscious of the fact that they had choices open to them and that they could take a negative path, which they had witnessed among family members, friends, or other young people with care experience. Mentors were described as role models, with young people highlighting aspects of their character, lifestyle or family life that they admired and would like to emulate.

Edel contrasted her own experience in care with that of her brother, just a year younger than her. She feels that her involvement with BBBS and Foróige provided the mentors in her life that helped her to choose a different life path than her brother. As highlighted in the previous section, Edel has developed an identity as an active citizen and is motivated to pursue a college degree in the social care arena.

> We went through the same experience, say I've actually moved more than him, so like . . . you'd think I'd be the one who would be more 'off the rails' but I always had Foróige. . . . And see now I'd be like planning to do my leaving cert and work for this organisation that has given me so much because I want to give back whereas he dropped out of, he's been expelled from two schools. . . . And like he has no role models, no mentors. . . . I don't think he had anyone to tell him this is wrong, this is right.
>
> (Edel, 17)

Rachel's story of changing her mindset with regard to education and going on to college was recounted earlier. Rachel says that there is no doubt but that she would have taken a different path if it was not for BBBS.

> I'm the youngest of six. So there is two boys and the rest of us are all girls and they are all pregnant at 16 or they have gotten someone pregnant at 16. . . . They are stay at home mams with no degrees, no leaving cert, there is nothing for them to fall back on. That would

have been me, or be down the whole drug line or alcohol line or do you know?

(Rachel, 21)

She also described how she prefers not to acknowledge her Traveller background, something that her mentor Eve and the BBBS Project Officers are helping her to 'work on'.

Once I became part of Big Brothers Big Sisters, they always encouraged me to embrace the fact that this is your background and embrace that this is where you have come from but I just rather ignore it and just pretend it didn't happen. . . . So that's still something we're working on.

(Rachel, 21)

Sarah eloquently described the pain associated with loneliness and disruption she experienced in her life, following her move to Ireland and subsequent entry into care. She described how having Ciara in her life helped her to choose a way of processing her experiences and choosing a way of coping that was positive rather than negative.

You're isolated and like when you become isolated it's like you're in this place, it's like you're in the dark basically you know? And like it's like there is no way out you know? . . . And like the circumstances of moving from my family home like any traditional setting in to like a care house is like this is a drastic change for me. Some people don't know how to process that. . . . So then if you can't process it then you can go to drinking. . . . Then you become that person like, aw it's all dark and there's no way out. So Ciara was that way out for me. You know? So it's like there is positive, there's more, you know?

(Sarah, 24)

Sarah spoke of how her relationship with her mentor, Ciara, has been instrumental in preparing her to engage confidently with society and to get better at 'knowing who I am'. Sarah said that she now does not let her skin colour hold her back in a way that she has observed among her friends.

It has really helped me, really built me up, really prepared me to be able to interact with other people. You can have somebody that can actually talk to you in such a way that you're like ok. . . . I can actually be great you know? . . . Just building myself and knowing who I am and being confident with that person. . . . Some of my friends still today they have like, they sometimes have those kind of issues like oh I can't get a job because I'm black. But for me I'm like, no, I will get a job regardless of what skin I have you know what I mean? So I guess if I didn't know her I'd probably have the same mind-set.

(Sarah, 24)

Sean spoke about how he had discussed the issues of alcohol and drugs with his mentor and decided to adopt a moderate approach to alcohol because of his awareness of how it could impact on his life. In his narratives, there is an awareness that he has agency in choosing a life path.

> We were talking about; like I've an interest in the law and about how people are always in trouble because of drink and drugs. We were just talking about that and he'd say I hope you don't do that sort of stuff. I've a friend; he – well I haven't talked to him now in a few years but he was, he used to live in the town here. He was fostered as well and he got in trouble there a couple of months ago. He's going to jail now and everything. He was drunk or he was doing drugs or something and it just messed him up completely.
>
> (Sean, 18)

Many of the research participants spoke of seeing their mentor as a role model, looking up to them for a variety of reasons, including their family life, career, work ethic or involvement in sports. For example, Rachel said that she always looked up to Eve, whom she had previously known as a youth worker, before she became her mentor. She sees in Eve a vision for how she would like her life to be, involving a job she loves, her own home and independence from social services.

> When I first met her, she had just come out of college and she was all happy because she had her college degree and she had her job and then as time went on she got married and she had kids. . . . So it's just, she was always someone I looked up to because she's always just I don't know, that's what I want to do. . . . Just a normal life so I'm not constantly between social workers or homes . . . to have my own house, my own job, my own degree, no one to have to go and get things from.
>
> (Rachel, 21)

Sean referred to his admiration for his mentor, Stephen, who had set up his own business and is doing very well with 'a new Beamer every year'. Sean's foster family are also self-employed so he has become used to this way of life and plans to start an apprenticeship for a trade soon. He said that he chooses not to be around people who 'sit around giving out', preferring the company of 'people that's working and I can have the craic [fun] with'.

> He was a great influence with his company like. He done really well with that, he's very successful. . . . He's saying like just get through your apprenticeship and go out on your own as soon as you can.
>
> (Sean, 18)

The findings in relation to transition and identity are summarised in Table 6.4.

Table 6.4 Summary of themes arising in relation to transition and identity

What the young person was struggling with	How the mentoring relationship helped	How the young people feel they have benefited as a result of mentoring
Coming to terms with who I am as a person Deciding what I want from life and the person I want to be Getting access to opportunities to facilitate chosen life paths	A space to discuss and process who they are and where they want to go Seeing mentor as a role model/possible selves Discussions around risk behaviour	Clearer ideas about who they are/where they want to go in life Greater confidence No enduring influence on identity

6.6 Discussion

In this chapter, the perspectives of research participants on the benefits of mentoring in their lives were reviewed under the themes of social and emotional well-being, educational engagement and progression, social capital and civic engagement. Themes of transition and identity were prominent in the narratives of some of the older participants in particular, whereby mentors were seen to offer support to young people in making the transition to early adulthood and in developing a coherent sense of identity.

As we saw in Chapter 1, the study of resilience focuses on the ability of individuals to recover from stressful and traumatizing situations (Luthar, Cicchetti, & Becker, 2000; Masten, 2011).Studies have attributed resilience to the presence of protective factors that help to mitigate against the effects of disadvantage, including intelligence and problem-solving skills, external interests or attachments, support from non-familial adults and a defined purpose in life and sense of self-efficacy (Ungar, 2008). Therefore, resilience studies explore those protective factors, processes and the mechanisms that play a role in changing the negative effects of adverse life situations (Sulimani-Aidan, 2018). For Ann Masten, resilience doesn't come from rare or special qualities, but from the everyday magic of ordinary, normative human resources, in the minds, brains, bodies of children, in their families and relationships and in their communities. (2001, p. 235). The findings of this research indicate that the 'everyday magic' of a mentoring relationship can bolster the coping resources and resilience of young people in care.

Having the support of parents and family is widely acknowledged as critical to coping and resilience in adolescence. Many young people in care will have experienced disconnections in their relationships with family and friends, which can cause individuals to feel less energetic, doubt their self-worth and be less inclined to seek new connections with others (Miller, 2008). Where the young person has the opportunity to re-establish meaningful connection with others, they start to feel understood and less alone (Jordan, 2013). The experiences of young people recounted in this study provide further evidence that conflict and breakdown in family relationships can leave young people feeling isolated and misunderstood and undermine their capacity to cope. Previous studies have shown that fostering new supportive relationships with adult figures and strengthening existing relationships with meaningful adults such as mentors are ways in which young people can increase their resilience (Sulimani-Aidan, 2018). For example, in their study among young people in residential care, Schofield et al. (2017) found that the development of nurturing relationships between staff and young people and a sense of 'family' were a key factor in the resilience of young people. Having ongoing support after leaving residential care, which helped them to move on with their lives but stay connected, was also significant.

In this study, we saw that young people valued the consistent support of their mentors, with some describing their mentor as being 'always there for me'. The young people who had made the transition to early adulthood were in a position to reflect back and see that their mentoring relationship had provided a secure base from which they could draw emotional, practical, advice and esteem support. These supportive relationships with their mentors continued after they had formally 'aged out' of the mentoring programme. For example, James, who is now in his early twenties, spoke of regularly meeting up with his mentor for a coffee if he is feeling stressed. Sean recently turned 18 but continues to meet his mentor for a weekly game of squash and a chat. Rachel is 24 and celebrates key family events with her mentor, including birthdays and Christmas. Having a supportive relationship with their mentor that they could call on if needed was a great source of comfort to many of the participants. Social workers taking part in a study by Sulimani-Aidan (2018) referred to the ability to lean on and reach out to others as one of the core aspects of successful coping despite adversity among young people in care.

As well as supporting coping by being present in the lives of young people on a consistent basis, mentors were also seen to support the development of specific coping abilities. It has been acknowledged that young people may need help with coping due to adversities and challenges faced before, during and when leaving care (Fernandez, 2009; Farmer, Selwyn, & Meakings, 2013). While there is no right or wrong way to cope, some strategies have been labelled as 'productive' and others as 'non-productive'. Frydenberg (2019) identifies non-productive coping strategies among adolescents as including withdrawal, anger, disengagement from school and engagement in risk behaviour, while productive coping includes dealing with problems, anger management and taking part in recreation or hobbies. As illustrated in Table 6.5, many of the research participants spoke of experiencing a lack of confidence, anxiety and anger issues, while some were socially isolated. Engaging with their mentor helped to bring them out of themselves and into

Table 6.5 Examples of how mentors supported young people to move from non-productive to productive coping strategies

Non-Productive coping	Productive coping
Keeping to self	Getting out, engaging with others
Bottling up feelings	Expressing their feelings
Angry outburst	Anger awareness and management
Ignoring a problem or seeing only the negatives	Focusing on the positive aspects of a situation
	Problem solving
Tension reduction through risk behaviour	Seeking relaxing diversions – e.g. sport, recreation, socialising
Disengaging from school and hobbies	Engaging with school and hobbies
Defeatist mindset	Growth mindset
Low social capital	Good social capital

Source: Adapted from Frydenberg, 2019, p. 45

the community, and provided a forum for them to have fun, talk about their feelings, express emotions and learn strategies for dealing with their emotions. Coping with emotions in a more productive way was pivotal in terms of facilitating the young person to engage more calmly and confidently with school, friends and career opportunities. Previous studies have shown that productive coping is associated with higher levels of emotional well-being while non-productive coping is associated with lower levels of emotional well-being and depression (McKenzie & Frydenberg, 2004; Frydenberg, 2019).

Frydenberg points out that disengagement from schooling can occur in the middle years of school when there are dips in the use of helpful coping strategies (2019, p. 81). She argues that a focus on developing good coping skills, school engagement, positive motivation and mindset are likely to lead to the most positive academic outcomes. We saw some examples in this study, such as those of Robin and Rachel, of disengagement from school. Research participants described how the intervention of mentors was effective in terms of helping them to process their feelings and to approach the situation with a more rational frame of mind. Mentors provided hands-on support with schoolwork and exam preparation, and acted as a sounding board for young people to think about what path they wanted to take in life. Through their mentoring relationships, the young people were exposed to environments and attitudes that placed a high value on education, psychological and emotional support to help them to keep going when they felt like giving up and practical support to enable them to succeed in education. A study by Mendis, Lehmann, and Gardner (2018) found that a conductive environment that avoids stigmatising children in care in relation to their learning and encouragement in all aspects of learning was important in supporting young people in care to succeed in education. Given that a key factor contributing to poor adult outcomes for children in care is lack of educational or vocational qualifications (Mendis et al., 2018), addressing the educational needs of care experienced young people is of critical importance (Brady et al., 2019).

A concept that is discussed in the context of coping is that of 'mindset', whereby having a particular mindset or set of beliefs about something can contribute to either productive or non-productive coping (Frydenberg, 2019). Yeager and Dweck (2012) found that a helpless performance mindset can lead to maladaptive thoughts, including avoidance of effort, whereas mastery focused young people, by contrast, focused on effort (Frydenberg, 2019). Some young people taking part in this study spoke about how they had come to change their mindset as a result of their relationship with their mentor. For example, Rachel spoke about changing her mindset regarding staying in education, while Sarah moved from a negative to a positive mindset in relation to not feeling disadvantaged because of her race and experiences of displacement. Edel came to see herself as someone with a lot to contribute to society, which provided her with the motivation to pursue a career in the social care arena. Sulimani-Aidan (2015) argues that future expectations are an important source of resilience for young people in care because they play a part in their goal planning and motivation to accomplish their goals. He argues that having positive expectations for the future can impact on young people's emotional status before leaving care, on their motivation to engage in programmes designed to help prepare them for independent adult life and affect their outcomes in adulthood.

Social capital is also identified as a productive coping strategy and a contributor to resilience. A number of the older participants described how they moved from low social capital to high social capital as a result of their involvement, with some reporting civic behaviour that grew from the social capital developed through the programme. This finding reflects the premise of relational cultural theory (RCT) that people in connected relationships are motivated to seek out connections with others, while, as a result of being active in the world, people feel more capable of acting within the world and do so (Miller, 2008; Horn & Spencer, 2018). As noted in Chapter 4, Liang, Spencer, West, and Rappaport (2013, p. 258) have proposed a shift in the mentoring field, 'from a "therapeutic" approach in which individual youth are the targets of the intervention to a more socially transformative approach wherein mentors and youth forge collaborative partnerships that promote positive youth development at individual and societal levels'. The model of mentoring adopted through this programme clearly extended beyond the one-to-one relationship and linked young people with a range of bonding and bridging social networks that they found to be empowering and supportive, including peers, adult volunteers and professional youth workers. Prieto-Flores and Gelis (2018) have pointed out that the outcomes from mentoring in terms of enhancing participation in community social activities, or in promoting acts of service to the community have not been given much attention in research to date. The findings of this study suggest that these outcomes can be significant for some young people.

A key aspect of resilience for children in care is accepting their life history and what has happened to them and being able to move on. Schofield et al. (2017, p. 783) note that young people in care face 'particular challenges in generating coherent narratives of complex family and care experiences . . . which would allow them to resolve feelings about the past and move on'. We saw in this study that young people valued the support of mentors to process and come to terms with difficult personal experiences. Mentors actively supported young people in this process of identity development, which also involved charting a course for the future and deciding the type of person they wanted to be. Some incorporated aspects of the mentor's lifestyle, character or achievements into their projections of their 'future selves' (Marcus & Nurius, 1986). Miller (2008) argues that participating in the relationship provides each person with a greater sense of self as well as a greater sense of the other.

6.7 Conclusion

In this chapter, the perspectives of research participants on the benefits of mentoring in their lives were reviewed and discussed. In Chapter 7, further findings from the research are outlined, this time focusing on the aspects of the mentor's approach or the mentoring relationship itself that the young people found helpful.

Summary messages

- Young people experienced great social and emotional well-being as a result of their mentoring relationship, including stress reduction, improved social skills, greater confidence and better ability to regulate their emotions.
- Mentoring relationships had a particular influence on educational outcomes and attainment for some young people taking part in the study.
- Some participants developed greater social capital and become involved in volunteering as a result of participation in the programme.
- Themes of transition and identity were prominent in the narratives of some of the older participants in particular, whereby mentors were seen to offer support to young people in making the transition to early adulthood and in developing a coherent sense of identity.
- The findings of this research indicate that the mentoring relationship worked to strengthen the coping resources and resilience of young people in care.

References

Brady, E., Gilligan, R., & Nic Fhlannchadha, S. (2019). Care-experienced young people accessing higher education in Ireland. *Irish Journal of Applied Social Studies, 19*(1), 5.

Christiansen, Ø., Havnen, K. J., Havik, T., & Anderssen, N. (2013). Cautious belonging: Relationships in long-term foster-care. *British Journal of Social Work, 43*(4), 720–738.

Cooley, C. H. (1902). *Human nature and the social order.* New York, NY: Charles Scribner's Sons.

Daly, F., & Gilligan, R. (2010). Selected educational outcomes for young people aged 17–19 years in long term foster care in Ireland. *How does foster care work: International evidence on outcomes* (pp. 243–257). London: Jessica Kingsley.

Erickson, E. H. (1968). *Identity: Youth and crisis.* London: Faber & Faber.

Farmer, E., Selwyn, J., & Meakings, S. (2013). 'Other children say you're not normal because you don't live with your parents'. Children's views of living with informal kinship carers: Social networks, stigma and attachment to carers. *Child & Family Social Work, 18*(1), 25–34.

Ferguson, K. M. (2006). Social capital and children's wellbeing: A critical synthesis of the international social capital literature. *International Journal of Social Welfare, 15*(1), 2–18.

Fernandez, E. (2009). Children's wellbeing in care: Evidence from a longitudinal study of outcomes. *Children and Youth Services Review, 31*(10), 1092–1100.

Field, J. (2008). *Social capital* (2nd ed., Key ideas). London and New York: Routledge.

Frydenberg, E. (2019). *Adolescent coping: Promoting resilience and well-being.* London: Routledge.

Healey, C. V., & Fisher, P. A. (2011). Young children in foster care and the development of favourable outcomes. *Children and Youth Services Review, 33*(10), 1822–1830.

Horn, J. P., & Spencer, R. (2018). Natural mentoring to support the establishment of permanency for youth in foster care. In E. Trejos-Castillo & N. Trevino-Schafer (Eds.), *Handbook of foster youth.* New York, NY: Routledge.

Innovations in Civic Participation. (2010). *Youth civic participation in action: Meeting community and youth needs worldwide.* Washington, DC: Innovations in Civic Participation.

Jordan, J. V. (2013). Relational resilience in girls. In S. Goldstein & R. Brooks (Eds.), *Handbook of resilience in children* (pp. 73–86). Boston, MA: Springer.

Liang, B., Spencer, R., West, J., & Rappaport, N. (2013). Expanding the reach of youth mentoring: Partnering with youth for personal growth and social change. *Journal of Adolescence, 36*(2), 257–267.

Luthar, S. S., Cicchetti, D., & Becker, B. (2000). The construct of resilience: A critical evaluation and guidelines for future work. *Child Development, 71*(3), 543–562.

Marcus, H., & Nurius, P. (1986). Possible selves. *American Psychologist, 41*, 954–969.

Masten, A. S. (2001). Ordinary magic: Resilience processes in development. *American Psychologist, 56*(3), 227.

Masten, A. S. (2011). Resilience in children threatened by extreme adversity: Frameworks for research, practice, and translational synergy. *Development and Sychopathology, 23*(2), 493–506.

McKenzie, V., & Frydenberg, E. (2004). Young people and their resources. In E. Frydenberg (Ed.), *Thriving, surviving or going under: Coping with everyday lives* (pp. 79–108). Greenwich, Connecticut: Information Age Publishing.

Mead, G. H. (1934). *Mind, self and society from the standpoint of a social behaviorist*. Chicago, IL: University of Chicago Press.

Mendis, K., Lehmann, J., & Gardner, F. (2018). Promoting academic success of children in care. *British Journal of Social Work, 48*(1), 106–123.

Miller, J. B. (2008). VI. Connections, disconnections, and violations. *Feminism & Psychology, 18*(3), 368–380.

Moran, L., McGregor, C., & Devaney, C. (2017). *Outcomes for permanence and stability for children in long-term care: Practice guidance*. Galway: UNESCO Child and Family Research Centre, Galway.

Prieto-Flores, Ò., & Gelis, J. F. (2018). What type of impact could social mentoring programs have? An exploration of the existing assessments and a proposal of an analytical framework. *Pedagogia Social, 31*, 149–162.

Putnam, R. D. (2000). *Bowling alone: The collapse and revival of American community*. New York, NY: Simon & Schuster.

Raposa, E. B., Erickson, L. D., Hagler, M., & Rhodes, J. E. (2018). How economic disadvantage affects the availability and nature of mentoring relationships during the transition to adulthood. *American Journal of Community Psychology, 61*(1–2), 191–203.

Rhodes, J. E. (2005). A model of youth mentoring. In D. L. DuBois & M. J. Karcher (Eds.), *Handbook of youth mentoring* (pp. 30–43). Thousand Oaks, CA: Sage Publications.

Rogers, J. (2017). 'Different'and 'Devalued': Managing the stigma of foster-care with the benefit of peer support. *British Journal of Social Work, 47*(4), 1078–1093.

Schofield, G., Larsson, B., & Ward, E. (2017). Risk, resilience and identity construction in the life narratives of young people leaving residential care. *Child & Family Social Work, 22*(2), 782–791.

Sulimani-Aidan, Y. (2015). Do they get what they expect? The connection between young adults' future expectations before leaving care and outcomes after leaving care. *Children and Youth Services Review, 55*, 193–200.

Sulimani-Aidan, Y. (2018). Promoting resilience among adolescents in care from their social workers' perspectives. *Children and Youth Services Review, 94*, 43–48.

Ungar, M. (2008). Resilience across cultures. *The British Journal of Social Work, 38*(2), 218–235.

Van Dam, L., Smit, D., Wildschut, B., Branje, S. J. T., Rhodes, J. E., Assink, M., & Stams, G. J. J. M. (2018). Does natural mentoring matter? A multilevel meta-analysis on the association between natural mentoring and youth outcomes. *American Journal of Community Psychology, 62*(1–2), 203–220.

Winter, K. (2012). Understanding and supporting young children's transitions into state care: Schlossberg's transition framework and child-centred practice. *British Journal of Social Work, 44*(2), 401–417.

Yeager, D. S., & Dweck, C. S. (2012). Mindsets that promote resilience: When students believe that personal characteristics can be developed. *Educational Psychologist, 47*(4), 302–314.

7 Youth perspectives on relational dynamics and quality in mentoring relationships

7.1 Introduction

In Chapter 6, young people's accounts of the benefits of mentoring in their lives were presented under the themes of social and emotional well-being, education, social capital and identity development. Continuing to draw on the primary research study, we now move on to examine young people's views on the characteristics of their mentors and of the mentoring relationship and their perspectives on how it differed from other relationships within their social network, particularly family, friends and social workers.

7.2 Helpful characteristics and relational qualities of mentors

As we saw in Chapter 4, there is a broad consensus in the mentoring literature that an essential ingredient in youth mentoring relationships is the development of a 'strong inter-personal connection, characterized by mutuality, trust and empathy' (Rhodes, 2005, p. 31).

The participants in the study alluded to a range of characteristics of their mentors and of their approaches that they found appealing and which helped them to become close. In general, mentors were described as being relaxed and easy to talk to. Some of the respondents said that while their mentor may have been older than them, it didn't feel like that because they were able to connect with them on their level.

> I could just chat about anything and everything basically.
>
> (Grace, 14)

> She was like another child. . . . Like she . . . loved these things like, she wouldn't be like strict or anything.
>
> (Robin, 18)

Part of the reason the mentors were seen as easier to talk to is that they generally do activities together that they both enjoy, which makes the conversation more relaxed and less pressurised.

> Like we were never really boring like we'd always do something fun, not just sit there and just talk about stuff. We'd make like bracelets in the hot chocolate shop and one time we did henna that you put on your hands.
>
> (Roisín, 15)

> Like say I met her the last day, she was helping me with my Ag. Science project and we just went for a drive around you know? Just talking about absolute nonsense.
>
> (Edel, 17)

Young people frequently referred to the fact that they and their mentors shared similar interests and characteristics which also made it easier to develop a rapport with them. Many of the research participants spoke about how well matched they were, with a number saying that they 'just clicked'. It is well established in the mentoring literature that mentoring pairs with similar interests and compatibility tend to produce more positive outcomes (De Wit, DuBois, Erdem, Larose, & Lipman, 2016; Gettings & Wilson, 2014). Lester, Goodloe, Johnson, and Deutsch (2019) found 'shared relational excitement' to be a characteristic of youth mentoring relationships characterised by mutuality. Within such relationships, not every interaction has to be deep and meaningful; rather 'a mix of surface-level interactions and vulnerable moments occur on a foundation of trust, which combine to foster mutuality' (p. 152). Having shared interests can help the relationship to last longer and to be sustainable in the long term, as evidenced by Sean and Stephen, who will continue to meet for their weekly game of squash even after their match is formally ended by the programme.

> We had the same personality and stuff. . . . She enjoyed sports and I do too like.
>
> (Maeve, 14)

> Well we both love cats, that's the biggest one, like she has a cat as well but I have loads of cats as well, we, like that's the main, we love cats and coffee and like we don't have the same taste in clothes now at all. Like we argue a lot and have a different style of clothes.
>
> (Roisín, 15)

> Once we finish up with Big Brother Big Sister thing we're still going to meet and play squash as much as we can.
>
> (Sean, 18)

Many of the young people referred to the fact that their mentor was non-judgemental;'someone who you can talk to without being like afraid of them judging you' (Sophie). This quote from Mary (19) illustrates that a non-judgemental approach was important for her because she had experienced significant adversity in her life, which she was still coming to terms with. Edel also appreciated being taken seriously and not treated like a child.

MARY: Just sometimes you want to hang out with an adult rather than a child who will understand you better, do you know? And doesn't judge you.
INTERVIEWER: Right, do you think that's important, not judging you?
MARY: Yes. I've been through a lot like, you know?

> She wouldn't treat me like I was a child . . . she would listen to me and I feel like at the time, say if I was to say anything I'd be told to shut up and go away and stuff like that but she'd genuinely listen to you.
> (Edel, 17)

Trust is widely recognised in the literature as a key ingredient of positive mentoring relationships (Donlan, McDermott, & Zaff, 2017; Rhodes, 2005; Spencer, 2006). The participants in this study highlighted trust in their mentor as an important relational quality. James describes how he trusted his mentor from the start, while Sarah describes how interactions with her mentor, Ciara, over time reinforced her belief that she was somebody who could be trusted.

> I trusted him straightaway; you just know when someone is a good person.
> (James, 21)

> Just having a conversation and then giving her own input to say ok yes, that's a good idea, oh that's not a good idea and just casual. It wasn't, there was no intent, there was no kind of like negative intention behind it so I trusted her. . . . I just knew that I could rely and trust her because she showed herself time and time again that she is trustworthy.
> (Sarah, 24)

> Even like the most stupid thing like a problem with a boy or like something really serious with my family and stuff like that I'd 100% trust her.
> (Edel, 17)

Empathy, which is described simply as understanding the other person's frame of reference, or 'stepping into their shoes' is considered a 'key ingredient' in youth mentoring relationships (Spencer, 2018; Rhodes, 2005). Sophie

(14) described feeling empathy from her mentor and saw the willingness of her mentor to share her experiences as helping to build trust. Edel spoke of how her mentor supported her with stress in her life but also took delight in sharing her successes and was genuinely 'proud' of her. Lester et al. (2019, p. 147) describe this process as 'experiential empathy 'the process through which mentors connect with, advise, and normalize the experiences of their mentees by sharing their own relevant experiences'.

INTERVIEWER: And what do you think did they do anything in particular to build trust do you think or how did the trust come about?
SOPHIE: So say if you were nervous about something. They'd be like oh I used to be nervous too and you know? They just tell you their stories as well and it's not just you like talking and talking to them like. It would be like you would mix in you know? It would be smooth. . . . It would make things a lot better seeing it from what they were like as well and like their different things that they did and stuff.

> She's always like so proud of you for doing anything like. You could be like 'oh I got an A in my test' and she'd be like oh my god now we have to go for hot chocolate . . . different things like that.
>
> (Edel, 17)

For Robin, honesty or authenticity was as an important characteristic in her mentor. She liked that her mentor would not pretend to like something just because Robin did but would be truthful with her opinions. Spencer (2006) considers authenticity on the part of mentors as essential to the change process because it ensures that the mentees are more likely to open up and express their feelings. Similarly, Donlan et al. (2017) found honesty to be critical to the building of trust in youth mentoring relationships.

> She was honest. . . . If I said like something and she would be like oh I'm not really into that or do you know like? That kind of thing.
>
> (Robin, 18)

International research with children in care has highlighted the importance of continuity as a key factor influencing the stability of children in care and leaving care (Refaeli, Mangold, Zeira, & Köngeter, 2017; Moran, McGregor, & Devaney, 2017). As we saw in Chapter 5, many of the mentoring relationships endured for much longer than the programme minimum of one year. Some of the research participants had experienced multiple transitions and many changes of social worker which meant that they did not experience continuity in support. The young people emphasised the consistency of support available from their mentors; the term 'always there' was used frequently. Mentors had clearly conveyed to these young people that they were important to them and that they could be relied on in times of need.

> It's just any time you need them, they're there regardless of what it is.
> (Rachel, 21)

> She was always there for me and if ever I needed to talk to anyone she was always there for me to talk to.
> (Grace, 14)

> INTERVIEWER: What do you think makes a good Big Brother?
> SEAN: Someone who has time to talk to you and is always there to talk to you. Like I could text Stephen now and he'd be there to talk even though he probably would be working he'd still try his best to talk to me.
> (Sean, 18)

A number of participants alluded to the techniques used by mentors to support mentees to make decisions. Rachel in particular was very aware of how her mentors had supported and respected her autonomy in making her own decisions. For example, when talking about how her mentor had convinced her not to leave school, Rachel showed an awareness of why her approach worked for her whereas others had failed. Rachel's narrative highlights that she had felt 'belittled' or disempowered in her interactions with other adults. This resonates with previous findings that mentoring styles are important in impacting youth's outcomes (Podmore, Fonagy, & Munk, 2014).

> They have a way, they: don't give out to you for doing things, they try and listen, which as a child everyone just shouts their perspective at you but they actually sit you down, they just listen to you and your perspective and they don't discourage you just because you're a child or just because you don't know what you're on about. . . . They don't belittle you I suppose is the best word to use. They just treat you like any normal person. They do a pros and a cons and they literally push you towards the pros but you make the decision yourself but they will give you all the information you need to make that decision and then encourage you to make that decision . . . and they won't stop until you do make that decision.
> (Rachel, 21)

> And I love that she [mentor] is like 'it's your decision'. Because if I said that to a social worker, like if social workers were running this and if I said that to a social worker they'd be like no you have to go.
> (Roisín, 15)

7.3 Helpful features of the BBBS programme

For Lily, the voluntary nature of the programme was a key factor; taking part was something she chose to do rather than being forced to do as had been the case with other experiences in her life. There is a sense that she feels stigmatised by her care experience and appreciates the opportunity to have a social space outside of 'all the care stuff'. The fact that it is separate to social services is clearly important to her.

> Being in Big Brother Big Sister . . . it is a choice. It's not like you're forced into doing it. Like first of all I was forced into care and . . . I didn't want to be in care. It's not forced . . . it's my thing. It's my little thing that I need that I don't want no one else, no one else has to be involved, no one else has to know like. And like Olivia isn't part of that thing, them things in my life like. . . . She is a part of my life but she's not part of like all the drama, all the care stuff that I go through. . . . And it's just someone I can talk to about literally anything.

While it was not specifically asked in the interviews, some of the young people referred to their mentors having backgrounds in youth work, teaching or social care. For example, Rachel's, Sarah's, James's and Edel's mentors were all youth or social care workers and their narratives suggest that having this skill set was of benefit in supporting them with very difficult and complex personal journeys. In addition to friendship and emotional support, their mentors connected them with a range of opportunities and resources that were of benefit to them and advocated for them where needed. It is also possible that their mentoring relationship lasted longer because their mentors worked in this area. As we saw in Chapters 3 and 4, there is a growing body of evidence that youth mentoring relationships (both natural and formal) are more beneficial when the mentor has experience in helping roles or professions (Jarjoura, Tanyu, Forbush, Herrera, Keller, 2018; Van Dam et al., 2018; Raposa et al., 2019; Raposa, Rhodes, & Herrera, 2016). However, this should not be interpreted as suggesting that mentors with other backgrounds were not successful but highlights that mentors with this profile may bring an additional skill set and capacity to link young people with beneficial social, psychological and educational resources.

It is also important to highlight that, as we saw in Chapter 6, many of the young people referred to support they received from BBBS Project Officers and Foróige and not just their mentors. Keller (2005) has conceptualised the mentoring relationship as a systemic model, arguing that the wider programme staff can play a direct role in reinforcing the positive processes occurring in the mentoring relationship, through connecting the young person to meaningful opportunities. Keller suggests that the overall effect of the mentoring intervention on the child's well-being may be 'the consequence of establishing a cohesive alliance' of caring adults who collectively support the child's development' (2005, p. 183). This process was particularly evident in the case of Edel, who referred to Foróige as her 'family' and had accessed a broad range of participation and leadership opportunities over many years. It could be argued that the core mentoring relationship is a mechanism through which young people are introduced to 'mentor rich environments' where they can develop natural relationships with supportive adults (Economic and Social Research Council [ESRC], 2007; Brady & Dolan, 2009).

7.4 The role of the mentor in the context of the young person's social network

Taking part in a youth mentoring programme means that a new adult is introduced to the young person's social network. Some unease has been expressed in the research literature regarding attempts to 'artificially' alter a young person's social network. Cutrona (2000), writing about social support more generally, cautions that attempts to 'graft on' a new member of a social network is a hazardous task, while Colley (2003) argues that the efforts of mentoring programmes to do so may undermine existing sources of support. Likewise, Philip (2003) argues that there has been uncertainty expressed regarding the impact of mentoring on existing social networks and how existing social networks interact with mentoring interventions.

One of the aims of this study was to explore young people's perceptions of where the mentoring relationship fits in terms of their social network. Given that young people in care can have a wide range of professionals involved in their lives, it could be argued that introducing another 'outsider' into their social network is inadvisable. As part of the research, therefore, participants were asked how their relationship with their mentor was different from relationships with family and friends and with social workers. In general, the relationship with their mentor was seen as different and complementary, providing a type of support that they were not accessing in their pre-existing social network.

With regard to family, respondents said that the key difference was that they could talk to their mentor about things that they might not feel comfortable talking to family about.

> You could tell her [mentor] different stuff that you wouldn't really tell them.
>
> (Chloe, 15)

> So Fiona [mentor] if you like is more of a sister to me than like, I know it's kind of bad to say now but I feel like I'm closer to Fiona than the rest of them so, because I can just talk to her about everything. Do you know in the family now I'd be kind of holding back saying a few stuff like and ranting to them but with Fiona I can just rant.
>
> (Roisín, 15)

Asked how their mentor was different from their friends, many of the research participants stressed the capacity of the mentor to understand, to listen and to be able to help. Roisin referred to her mentor Fiona as having better capacity to read a situation and offer good advice than her friends who 'could be silly about it'. Referring to the feedback and guidance she got from Ciara, her mentor, with her spoken English, Sarah said that this was not support she felt she would have received from her friends because they would not have understood that it was important to her. Likewise, Mary said that friends your own age can be immature so it is good to have a trusted older adult to turn to for advice.

> It's just sometimes people your own age could be really immature like when you ask certain questions and stuff. It's good to have someone who has so much in common with you and then be able to have that trust to ask something.
>
> (Mary, 19)

A number of research participants, including Sophie and Edel, spoke about the lack of trust that can be present in peer relationships, which makes it valuable to have a trusted person to talk to who is removed from these networks.

> Sometimes . . . if you're in a group of friends you kind of have to like, in this day and age you have to put like . . . not a cover, but you have to be in a certain way sometimes . . . or you're afraid to say something and like if you're having a bad day at home like and you don't want to talk about it to your parents you know? You'd be afraid to talk about that to your friend because you didn't want them to be like judging you or anything like that but when you have a Big I feel like because they're like an adult and they know these problems like, you are able to like talk from your point of view and like they can tell you that like, oh yes, that's completely understandable you know? Because they know . . . what it would be like if you had certain problems.
>
> (Sophie, 14)

> I suppose like with my school friends because I moved to two different schools I wouldn't know them as well say as, you could know them for years, I don't know what they're saying about me to you know? Each other, that kind of way. . . . You'd hear something that you told someone going around and then you're kind of like, oh, especially in the school I'm in now, like you're like, but you'd say something to Joan [mentor] and that's it.
>
> (Edel, 17)

Because the relationship with social workers and social services is a significant one for young people in care and their families (McEvoy & Smith,

2011; Moran et al., 2017), it could be assumed that young people in care could access social support from their social workers and that a mentor would not be required. In this study, therefore, we also explored how the research participants felt that their relationship with their mentor compares to their relationship with their social workers. The findings indicate that the majority of young people see their relationship with their mentors as having the characteristics of a naturally formed friendship, whereas relationships with social workers are viewed more as a professional-client relationship. For Mary (19), the key difference was that 'it was like a friend more so than like an official kind of a thing that you had to do and it was just more laid back, more chilled out really'. Sarah (24) said that she and her siblings dealt with a lot of social workers from when they were taken into care. For her, the key difference between her relationship with social workers and her mentor was that the mentoring relationship was private and would not be documented and shared with others. The tendency of social workers to take notes during meetings was also cited by Lily and Roisín as a barrier to their opening up.

> So because we were dealing with a lot of social workers and stuff like that so most of the time it was basically, the conversation was written down but for Ciara [mentor] it wasn't something like, when I would meet her it's not for her to document, to put into a file and then give to somebody else and then it wasn't like that, so I was comfortable in you know?
>
> (Sarah, 24)

Many of the participants said that they find it easier to talk to their mentor than they would to a social worker. Sean said that he had three social workers during his time in care and that while some of them were nice, he 'just didn't connect with them' and would not share anything personal with them, whereas he would talk to Stephen his mentor 'about anything'. He found it hard to pinpoint precisely what the difference was but said that there is 'something about him [his mentor] – I just trust him more than I would have trusted social workers'. Sean said that social workers are 'more formal and official about it' whereas he saw his mentor as 'someone that can understand what I'm talking about'. In a similar vein, Robin said about her mentor that 'you can just tell her things I think' but she would 'feel different saying it to her [social worker]'. One of the reasons Robin found it easier to talk was 'because you got to go out to do stuff and then you weren't just sitting there talking . . . so you're not just sitting there being shy, like agreeing with everything they say'.

Some young people alluded to what they perceived to be a lack of empathy from their social workers. Grace said that 'social workers hear it all the time so they don't really care'. This comment suggests that because the social worker has many clients, their capacity to care for each individual is diminished. Rachel expressed the view that social workers are not there if you need them, but get in touch if they need something. Both Roisín and Edel felt passionately that social workers don't listen to the perspective of the young person and would be more likely to listen to the foster carer. They both value the fact that their mentors are just focused on them, which makes them more likely to confide in them and trust them.

> She [mentor] doesn't really care about [foster Mother] or my Mum. She just is focused on me, what I have to say and like everything that I say, so in that way I'd be like more inclined to go for Fiona than the rest of them.
>
> (Roisín, 15)

Some of the participants expressed anger in relation to frequent changes of social worker that they had experienced, an issue which has previously been highlighted in Irish research studies with children in care (McEvoy & Smith, 2011, p. 24; Jackson, Brady, Forkan, Tierney, & Kennan, 2018). For example, Lily had experienced a lack of continuity with regard to social workers in her life; her current social worker is the seventh one she has had during her time in care. She said that she associates social workers with 'stress' and doesn't feel she can rely on them for support. Lily's experience reflects the findings of Skoog, Khoo, and Nygren (2015) which highlight that a lack of continuity in relationships with social workers can have a negative emotional impact on young people in care.

7.5 Discussion

As we saw in Chapter 1, a key argument of relational cultural theory (RCT) is that, because humans are 'hard-wired to connect', meaningful relationships with others throughout the life course are critical for psychological health and well-being. Young people who have experienced disconnections in their relationships with others can retreat inwards and may be reluctant to seek out new connections. Efforts to forge new relational connections in a formal sense, such as through a youth mentoring programme, are complex and must ensure that the support provided is compatible with the personality and interests of the young person (Cutrona, 2000). The relationship is more likely to be seen as meaningful and social support more readily accepted if the young persons feel they have something in common with the other person, feel close to them, can rely on them to deliver the required support and feel that they are honest and authentic. The support giver should be not perceived by the recipient as patronising or demeaning in any way; on the contrary, they should hold the young person in high esteem (Bolger & Amarel, 2007; Dolan & Brady, 2012). It also important that the relationship is characterised by mutuality; for example, that the young person is not just a recipient of help but participates equally in an inter-dependent relationship.

In this chapter, we turned our attention to young people's perceptions of the quality of the support provided in their mentoring relationships, attempting to identify the characteristics of the mentoring relationship or mentor's approach identified as helpful or meaningful. The relational dynamics and characteristics identified by young people as helpful are broadly reflective of findings in the social support literature as well as the wider mentoring literature.

The language used by young people to describe their mentors – easy-going, relaxed, non-judgemental, someone you could trust, empathetic, honest and authentic is also consistent with the definition of growth-promoting relationships identified in relational cultural theory (Jordan, 2013; Miller, 2008).

Young people also valued the consistency and continuity of support available from their mentors. The social support literature highlights that the security of perceiving that someone is 'there for you' if you need him or her can be as important as the actual support received (Cutrona, 2000). For these young people, the mere existence of the relationship in itself was perceived as beneficial. Mentors were also described as supporting young people's agency and autonomy, encouraging them to make decisions for themselves. This style is in keeping with the relational mentoring model (Fletcher & Ragins, 2007, p. 375), whereby the mentor does not have 'power over' but exercises 'power with' and 'power for' the mentee. The literature on coping emphasises that people generally do better where they are given the opportunity to assess and guide their own development (Frydenberg, 2019), while the social ecology of resilience emphasises the relationships between individual agency and wider social context in influencing resilience for young people in care (Berridge, 2017). In this study, young people identified the non-directive approach as a critical feature of mentoring because it gave them the space and scaffolding to articulate their feelings and take action to address their own issues. This is of particular importance for children in care, who can often feel powerless in the context of their own lives (Jackson et al., 2018). Lily articulated this very well when she said that very little in her life so far has been her choice. For her, taking part in mentoring was a positive expression of her own agency; agency which was further facilitated through her activities and interests she pursued while taking part in the programme. Brady, Dolan, and Canavan (2017) have argued that youth mentoring programmes can allow time and space for young people to access tangible help and emotional sustenance that in turn can help them to pursue their own interests, needs and objectives.

We also saw in the responses that young people had an intuitive awareness of the strengths and shortcomings of the support provided in their social networks and could discern added value or complementarity of the mentor in comparison with family and friends. They saw the value of the mentor as being 'outside' of their daily lives, a trusted and wise adult they could talk to in a way that they couldn't talk to others in their worlds.

It was apparent that for some, relationships with family and friends were not characterised by closeness and trust (Cotterel, 2007). As we saw in the previous chapter, one of the roles of the mentor was to help young people to deal with stress and conflict arising in these relationships, thus helping them to maintain and prevent breakdowns in their existing social network. Dolan and Brady (2012) have argued that it is important that young people have a range of sources of social support rather than having all their 'eggs in one basket'. If there is one sole source of help for a young person and if the relationship ends (i.e. the supporter dies or there is a breakdown in their relationship) the youth can find him or herself left with no other source of help (Dolan & Brady, 2012).

The study also provides some interesting insights into young people's perceptions of the role of informal relationships vis-à-vis formal relationships in social care. Because social workers have statutory responsibility with regard to child protection, young people don't have a choice with regard to engagement with them and can often feel embarrassed and stigmatised by having child welfare workers involved in their lives (Sutton & Stack, 2013; Serbinski & Brown, 2017). Furthermore, professionals such as social workers can be constrained in their capacity to form close, authentic relationships with young people because they must be attentive to the perspectives of other stakeholders, such as birthparents, foster parents and supervisors (Philip, 1997). Voluntary mentors occupy a different 'space' and have the freedom to focus their full attention on the young person. The research participants saw clear differences between mentors and social workers, highlighting that mentors, in contrast to social workers, 'don't write things down', give them their full attention, are empathetic, support autonomous decision making and provide consistent support. These findings are in line with previous research which found that young people can be reluctant to share their problems with formal helpers because they fear their problems will not be kept confidential (Hallet, Murray, & Punch, 2003). Markward, McMillan, and Markward (2003) found that youth often experienced relationships with institutional agents, such as teachers, as depersonalising and denigrating and preferred those who used a 'lighter' or more humorous approach. It can be argued that the findings indicate that mentors are seen by young people as part of the 'life world' which refers to the lived realm of informal, culturally grounded interactions, whereas social workers are seen to represent the 'system world', which is composed of formal organizations, such as governments, private companies, unions, and courts (Habermas, 2015). Another interpretation is that the approach of social workers was viewed by young people as 'instrumental' (i.e. focused on problem solving) in contrast to the 'presence approach', whereby the volunteer is 'there for others' without focusing directly on problem solving (Baart, 2002). According to Baart (2002), presence practitioners take time to get to know the person and his or her environment deeply and strive to affirm the fundamental dignity of the person. While not being problem focused, these approaches may lead to problem solving.

7.6 Conclusion

In Chapter 6, mentoring relationships were seen to support young people in care in the areas of social and emotional well-being, education, social capital and identity development. In this chapter, we explored the characteristics and relational qualities of mentors that young people viewed as important or helpful. Mentors were described as relaxed, having shared interests, compatible personalities and being non-judgemental. Mentors were also associated with empathy, honesty, continuity and supporting autonomous decision making. The voluntary nature of the BBBS programme and the fact that mentors often had relevant experience of youth work or social care were identified as important by some. Young people see their relationships with their mentors as akin to a naturally formed friendship, whereas relationships with social workers were described more in terms of a professional-client relationship. In Chapter 8, we bring together the insights from this chapter, with learning from the book so far to discuss the key messages and practice implications that emerged in relation to youth mentoring for children in care.

Summary points: relational dynamics and quality in mentoring relationships

- Young people described mentors as easy-going, relaxed, having similar interests to them, non-judgemental, someone you could trust, empathetic, honest and authentic. Mentors were also described as supporting autonomous decision making.
- Some mentors had backgrounds in youth work or social care, which meant that they could connect young people with resources and opportunities of benefit to them.
- In addition to the support of their mentors, many young people drew on the support of the wider BBBS programme and Foróige.
- A mentor is viewed as providing an alternative form of non-judgemental social support to family and peers and this is of especial importance for children in care when their wider network relationships can be disrupted and/or difficult.
- Young people differentiate between mentor relationships and social work relationships in terms of level of formality and degree of empathy they experience.

References

Baart, A. (2002). *The presence approach: An introductory sketch of a practice.* Paper Series Catholic Theological University, Utrecht.

Berridge, D. (2017). The education of children in care: Agency and resilience. *Children and Youth Services Review*, 77, 86–93.

Bolger, N., & Amarel, D. (2007). Effects of social support visibility on adjustment to stress: Experimental evidence. *Journal of Personality and Social Psychology*, 92(3), 458–475.

Brady, B., & Dolan, P. (2009). Youth mentoring as a tool for community and civic engagement: Reflections on findings of an Irish research study. *Community Development*, 40(4), 359–366.

Brady, B., Dolan, P., & Canavan, J. (2017). 'He told me to calm down and all that': A qualitative study of social support types in a youth mentoring programme. *Child and Family Social Work*, 2(1), 266–274.

Colley, H. (2003). *Mentoring for social inclusion*. London: Routledge Falmer.

Cotterell, J. (2007). *Social networks in youth and adolescence* (2nd ed., Adolescence and Society). London and New York, NY: Routledge.

Cutrona, C. E. (2000). Social support principles for strengthening families. In J. Canavan, P. Dolan, & J. Pinkerton (Eds.), *Family support: Direction from diversity* (pp. 103–122). London: Jessica Kingsley.

De Wit, D. J., DuBois, D., Erdem, G., Larose, S., & Lipman, E. L. (2016). The role of program-supported mentoring relationships in promoting youth mental health, behavioral and developmental outcomes. *Prevention Science*, 17(5), 646–657.

Dolan, P., & Brady, B. (2012). *A guide to youth mentoring: Providing effective social support*. London: Jessica Kingsley.

Donlan, A. E., McDermott, E. R., & Zaff, J. F. (2017). Building relationships between mentors and youth: Development of the TRICS model. *Children and Youth Services Review*, 79, 385–398.

Economic and Social Research Council. (2007). *Researching youth mentoring – Building theory and building evidence (ESRC Seminar Series on Mentoring and Social Policy)*. Aberdeen, UK: Rowan Group.

Fletcher, J. K., & Ragins, B. R. (2007). Stone center relational cultural theory: A window on relational mentoring. In B. R. Ragins & K. E. Kram (Eds.), *The handbook of mentoring at work: Theory, research, and practice* (pp. 373–399). Thousand Oaks, CA: Sage Publications.

Frydenberg, E. (2019). *Adolescent coping: Promoting resilience and well-being*. London: Routledge.

Gettings, P. E., & Wilson, S. R. (2014). Examining commitment and relational maintenance in formal youth mentoring relationships. *Journal of Social and Personal Relationships*, 31(8), 1089–1115.

Habermas, J. (2015). *The theory of communicative action: Lifeworld and systems, a critique of functionalist reason* (Vol. 2). Hoboken, NJ: John Wiley & Sons.

Hallet, C., Murray, C., & Punch, S. (2003). Young people and welfare: Negotiating pathways. In C. Hallett & A. Prout (Eds.), *Hearing the voices of children: Social policy for a new century*. London: Routledge Falmer.

Jackson, R., Brady, B., Forkan, C., Tierney, E., & Kennan, D. (2018). *Collective participation of children in care: A formative evaluation of the Tusla/EPIC foster care action groups*. Galway: UNESCO Child and Family Research Centre, NUI Galway.

Jarjoura, G. R., Tanyu, M., Forbush, J., Herrera, C., Keller, T., American Institutes for Research (AIR), & United States of America. (2018). *Evaluation of the mentoring enhancement demonstration program: Technical report*. Washington, DC: American Institutes for Research.

Jordan, J. V. (2013). Relational resilience in girls. In S. Goldstein & R. Brooks (Eds.), *Handbook of resilience in children* (pp. 73–86). Boston, MA: Springer.

Keller, T. E. (2005). A systemic model of the youth mentoring intervention. *Journal of Primary Prevention*, 26(2), 169–188.

Lester, A. M., Goodloe, C. L., Johnson, H. E., & Deutsch, N. L. (2019). Understanding mutuality: Unpacking relational processes in youth mentoring relationships. *Journal of Community Psychology*, 47(1), 147–162.

Markward, M., McMillan, L., & Markward, N. (2003). Social support among youth. *Children and Youth Services Review*, 25(7), 571–587.

McEvoy, O., & Smith, M. D. (2011). *Listen to our voices! Hearing children and young people living in the care of the state*. Dublin: Government Publications.

Miller, J. B. (2008). VI. Connections, disconnections, and violations. *Feminism & Psychology*, 18(3), 368–380.

Moran, L., McGregor, C., & Devaney, C. (2017). *Outcomes for permanence and stability for children in long-term care: Practice guidance*. Galway: UNESCO Child and Family Research Centre, Galway.

Philip, K. (1997). *New perspectives on mentoring: Young people, youth work and adults* (Doctoral dissertation). University of Aberdeen.

Philip, K. (2003). Youth mentoring: The American dream comes to the UK? *British Journal of Guidance & Counselling*, 31(1), 101–112.

Podmore, B., Fonagy, P., & Munk, S. (2014). *Characterizing mentoring programs for promoting children and young people's wellbeing*. Retrieved from www.annafreud.org/media/6019/characterising-mentoring-programmes.pdf

Raposa, E. B., Rhodes, J. E., & Herrera, C. (2016). The impact of youth risk on mentoring relationship quality: Do mentor characteristics matter? *American Journal of Community Psychology*, 57(3–4), 320–329.

Raposa, E. B., Rhodes, J., Stams, G. J. J., Card, N., Burton, S., Schwartz, S., . . . Hussain, S. (2019). The effects of youth mentoring programs: A meta-analysis of outcome studies. *Journal of Youth and Adolescence*, 1–21.

Refaeli, T., Mangold, K., Zeira, A., & Köngeter, S. (2017). Continuity and discontinuity in the transition from care to adulthood. *The British Journal of Social Work*, 47(2), 325–342.

Rhodes, J. E. (2005). A model of youth mentoring. In D. L. DuBois & M. J. Karcher (Eds.), *Handbook of youth mentoring* (pp. 30–43). Thousand Oaks, CA: Sage Publications.

Serbinski, S., & Brown, J. (2017). Creating connections with child welfare workers: Experiences of foster parents' own children. *British Journal of Social Work*, 47(5), 1411–1426.

Skoog, V., Khoo, E., & Nygren, L. (2015). Disconnection and dislocation: Relationships and belonging in unstable foster and institutional care. *The British Journal of Social Work*, 45(6), 1888–1904.

Spencer, R. (2006). Understanding the mentoring process between adolescents and adults. *Youth & Society*, 37(3), 287–315.

Spencer, R. (2018). *Empathy – A critical ingredient in youth mentoring relationships*. Retrieved from www.evidencebasedmentoring.org/empathy-a-critical-ingredient-in-youth-mentoring-relationships/

Sutton, L., & Stack, N. (2013). Hearing quiet voices: Biological children's experiences of fostering. *British Journal of Social Work*, 43(3), 596–612.

Van Dam, L., Smit, D., Wildschut, B., Branje, S. J. T., Rhodes, J. E., Assink, M., & Stams, G. J. J. M. (2018). Does natural mentoring matter? A multilevel meta-analysis on the association between natural mentoring and youth outcomes. *American Journal of Community Psychology*, 62(1–2), 203–220.

8 Mentoring for young people in care

Messages for policy and practice

8.1 Introduction

Having presented the key findings from the study which underpins this book with accompanying conceptual mapping of mentoring for children and youth care, this chapter moves to discuss the learning and signpost future directions for policy and practice. The evidence from existing literature and our current research findings provide a convincing argument that youth mentoring has value for young people in care. In this chapter, we emphasise this message and discuss the implications for practice from a series of perspectives. This includes a consideration of how child welfare and social work practice can be developed to maximise the use of mentoring for children in care through better planning and complementarity between formal and informal support services. Consideration is also given to implications for youth mentoring organisations. In addition to identifying the strengths of youth mentoring for children and youth in care, the risks and limitations of mentoring are strongly highlighted.

8.2 Youth mentoring has value for children in care

The key message from this book is that youth mentoring, both natural and formal, has value for young people in care. The influence of a mentoring relationship can extend beyond the mentor-mentee dyad to have an impact across the multiple settings of the young person's ecological context. Children and youth in care occupy a complex ecological context from micro to meso, exo and macro levels (e.g. Bronfenbrenner, 1986; Bronfenbrenner & Morris, 1998; Bronfenbrenner & Crouter, 1983; Hayes, Toole, & Halpenny, 2017). With regard to the four components of the ecological context – process, person, context and time – we can map how mentoring relationships can work for a young person in his or her environment. *Process* in this context refers to the use of mentoring as a non-formal or semi-formal support to supplement statutory provisions for children in state care. *Person* refers to the personality and the relational aspects that influence individuals' own development and their connections with others. *Context* relates to interactions between different levels of a young person's system from multiple micro level interactions (e.g. birth family, foster family, school) to meso level connections (e.g. interactions between family, friends, school) to exo level interactions (e.g. professionals, teachers, mentoring organisations, support workers) and macro level interactions with systems of law and policy (e.g. care monitoring and support processes, care order rules and regulations) that influence the day-to-day experience. *Time*, represented as the chrono level in Bronfenbrenner's ecological model, depicts key moments, changes over the life course and transitions. Young people in care can experience conflict and disconnections in their experiences across these systems, which can cumulate and cause further problems over time. The core premise of relational cultural theory (RCT), that healthy, close relationships are key to well-being, coping and thriving across the life course, sits very comfortably within an ecological framework. It can be argued, based on the evidence presented in this book, that a supportive growth promoting relationship with an adult mentor has the potential to enable young people in care to interact more seamlessly and with less conflict with the various elements of their eco-system.

Compared to many of their peers, young people in care have a range of formal professional services such as social care and social work practitioners involved in their lives. Dealing with a lot of adult professionals on an ongoing basis can be overwhelming and can lead to the young person having a feeling of being watched all the time (Stein, 2012). It could be assumed that introducing another adult into their lives would exacerbate these feelings. However, we saw in this research that young people in care viewed their mentors as providing a different type of support from social work or other professionals and different from family and friends. An important message is that the semi-formal role of the mentor allows greater potential for the development of a more trusting and empathetic relationship which young people need in order to be able to confide and seek support. Our study indicates that the majority of young people see the relationship with the mentor as having the characteristics of a naturally formed friendship, including a personal and mutual connection. One of the strongest cases for mentoring for young people, therefore, lies in the simple fact that it is provided by a friend who is deemed to be 'outside' of the care system and who does not know all the details pertaining to the life of the young person. Thus the mentor can act as a 'social valve' for the mentee by offering a non-judgemental listening ear where young persons can express themselves fully. This respite function of mentoring, which lies outside of formal service systems, can be an asset for young people in care. Young people described how having this outlet helped them to embrace more productive coping strategies in their various social contexts, including home, school and with peers. Thus, there is important learning about the value of mentoring that can lead to it being promoted more actively as an important supportive resource for young people during and after their time in care.

Reflecting the findings of previous research on mentoring, the research undertaken for this book found that young people viewed their mentoring relationship as enhancing their social and emotional well-being by providing a social outlet and a listening ear, relieving stress and improving sociability and self-confidence. Mentors were also seen to provide practical support and encouragement in relation to education, while also helping to scaffold young people's transition to adulthood. While mentoring is generally considered a one-to-one intervention, the findings showed that young people were facilitated to develop bonding and bridging social capital and become engaged in civic behaviour, including volunteering and youth leadership. While the research in this book focused on mentoring relationships created in the context of a formal programme, as we saw in Chapter 3, previous research has shown that natural and informal mentors can also play an important role in the lives of young people in care (Ahrens, Dubois, Richardson, Fan, & Lozano, 2008; Ahrens et al., 2011; Thompson, Greeson, & Brunsink, 2016). From a social support theory perspective, they provide the 'one significant adult' which is known to play such a crucial role in assisting young people in their development and transition to adulthood. Given the relatively poorer outcomes in the areas of health, well-being and education for children in care, it is important that the potential of youth mentoring is given due consideration.

While it can be beneficial or even transformative for some, it should be emphasised that a mentoring relationship is not a suitable option for all young people living in care. For some young people, the double adversity of experiencing family breakdown and then living in care, the expectation that they are ready for an additional new friendship may be simply too much for them. Some young people may be slow to trust others and prefer to keep a distance (Greeson, Garcia, Kim, Thompson, & Courtney, 2015). It should also be noted that youth mentoring is not always a success or a case of 'plain sailing'. Young people in foster care who are paired with volunteer mentors may be especially susceptible to relationship breakdown due to histories of disrupted attachments with parents or other caregivers (Spencer, Collins, Ward, & Smashnaya, 2010). Careful attention must therefore be paid to the practice considerations outlined later in this chapter. It may by that in some instances, mentoring is not suitable in itself but the ethos and principles of mentoring may still be relevant to inform practice developments.

8.3 Macro-level implications for social work and child welfare systems

While child welfare regimes in many countries have undergone significant transformation over recent decades, and there is some evidence of preventive interventions reducing the numbers of children in care, persistent evidence of poorer outcomes for children in care up to the present day can be seen as a chronic indictment of modern welfare systems. The future evidence of success will be the observation of a dramatic change in how young people in care describe and experience their interactions in their complicated and often multi-layered ecosystems. At a macro level, there is a need for wider system change that more dramatically orients itself towards prevention, parental and child participation and partnership working between all elements of the young person's ecosystem from micro to macro and informal to formal interactions to achieve better outcomes and best interests for children and young people. The compelling findings from young people, in our study and others, about the potential negative impact of some of the statutory child welfare processes must be addressed urgently.

Social work theory and practice is in a process of change and development and remains a 'moveable feast'. Many authors discuss the impact of neo-liberalism on social work (e.g. Hyslop, 2018) which brings mostly negative connotations associated with increased marketization of services, reduced budgets, managerialism and absence of sufficient focus on welfare, need and context. But there are other more positive influences shaping social work also such as a stronger emphasis on theory building and development as something not just for academic domains but for practitioners and service users to be actively involved in creating and activating (e.g McGregor, 2019). As discussed in Chapter 1 the Munro report of Child Protection in 2011 and reactions to it have led to a re-focus on the importance of relationships in child welfare practice. Recent research and literature especially in the United Kingdom have built on this theme of relationships and working in partnership with families and children. More broadly in social work, the need to move away from the dichotomy of expert-service user relationship towards more collaborative forms of practice is a major theme in current social work debates (see e.g. Golightley & Holloway, 2018; McGregor, 2019). Methods of co-production and the use of the recovery model where service users are seen as experts over their own direction are becoming more and more dominant as core social work methodologies.

Implicit within such democratisation and globalisation of social work, knowledge and theory is a shift away from the notion of the social worker as the expert and the client as the recipient of that expertise. This leads to a potential loosening of the relationship between so-called formal services and informal approaches. As argued in Chapter 1, what is often overlooked by professionals is the fact that the majority of social support that young people receive comes from their natural social networks of family and friends (Dolan & Brady, 2012). The evidence from literature and research considered in this book on the utilisation of youth mentoring is compelling as to its importance for nurturing informal and semi-formal support for children in care. But it must be acknowledged also that this balancing of formal, semi-formal and informal support is complex territory when it comes to specific social issues such as children and young people in statutory care face.

Yet, despite the present emphasis on participation, collaboration and partnership principles, there continues to be an overly fixed distinction between the 'formality' of social work theory and methods and the 'informality' of theory and method relating to volunteer and/or community based work carried out by 'non-experts' in that they are not qualified social workers or its equivalent (e.g. counsellor/therapist). While such distinction is needed to differentiate the complexities of different approaches used in social work and to clarify the statutory responsibilities for children in care vis-à-vis additional support services, an over-reliance on a narrow understanding of the divide between formal and informal blocks out the possible values involved in seeking to combine (formal) social work and (semi-formal/informal) youth mentoring. For example, even in situations where the nature of the social work relationship is bound by formalities of procedure and legal processes, there is potential for social work to be more proactive in seeking out and setting up mentoring for young people to supplement the often limited support that they can provide in their roles. Guidance in relation to such opportunities will be provided in the next section.

8.4 Guidance for child welfare practice

The value of enhancing collaborative work between the formal care support given through social work support for foster parents and children in care and youth mentoring models and programmes is strongly evidenced in this book. We now move on to identify some guidelines for child welfare practice with regard to youth mentoring.

Focus on the need for supportive relationships for young people in care: The importance of focusing on 'relationships' emerges strongly across the volume. We argue that the need for supportive relationships for the young person could and should be made more explicit in care planning and review processes. The young person in care must be at the centre at all times and the question asked about how strong and supportive relational interactions can be developed in a way that takes account of the many complex considerations with regard to support. However, in doing so, we have to be aware of the diversity of care-experienced young people. Many young people are helped by their relationship with foster parents, social workers and others, such as youth workers or teachers. Young people may not be on their own when they leave care as many reconnect with and live with extended family. Some young people connect with natural mentors in their own social networks (Ahrens et al., 2011). In some jurisdictions, young people are able to stay in the care system until the age of 21, and in education systems, which can result in better outcomes. It is important therefore in promoting the use of social support that we see it as much about recognising the strengths and resilience the young person has in their informal and natural environment, as well as looking at gaps and formal supports needed. Specifically it requires better use of methods such as social network analysis and ecosystem building to identify natural and willing supporters. There may be potential to support and strengthen existing mentoring relationships in the young person's social network.

Consider mentoring as an option for young people in care: For young people deemed to have gaps in their support needs, the possibility of youth mentoring should be considered and connections made with mentoring organisations to help forge these opportunities. As we have seen in this book, there are a number of options with regard to mentoring including identifying a mentor from within the young person's informal network or a mentor from a mentoring organisation who supports in a semi-formal capacity. Understanding the benefits and limits of different forms of mentoring is essential and an openness on the part of professionals and service providers to considering the type and range of mentoring as appropriate for the child or youth in care is key. In the first place, this requires professionals to be more proactive in promoting mentoring as a crucial supplementary support to a young person, and not to assume because a young person in care is facing multiple adversities at a given time that mentoring is not an option for her/him.

Recognise and value the contribution of mentoring within child welfare: In addition to using mentoring to strengthen access to a supportive relationship at the micro and meso levels, those also (and inevitably) involved with the child in care – the foster parent or residential care worker, the social worker, the team leader – need to be proactive in considering how these relational interactions can be valued and supported during and after a care experience. For example, Stelter, Kupersmidt, and Stump (2017) suggest that it may be useful to include natural mentors more formally in planning for the young person leaving care on the basis that they may have 'unique insights' into the young person's needs and may be able to offer ongoing support to help them to meet their goals. This is also modelled within the framework for other service provision for children and youth in care. For example in Family Group Conferences, natural mentors are identified and utilised as supporters for children youth and parents (Connolly & Masson, 2014). In doing this, a balance needs to be struck between maintaining the essence of mentoring as a semi-formal, relational process that is outside of the child care system, while also attempting to have good connections between the mentoring organisation/mentor and those working within the formal child care service. This may mean inclusion of mentors in care planning and review but most importantly *only* at the request of the young person. Ahrens et al. (2011) argue that it may be valuable to provide training specifically for mentors of young people in care that incorporates learning from research on the factors that influence relationship quality (engaging building and maintaining) and duration (how to keep the connection sustainable) for this group of young people. In doing this, however, the risk of the mentor becoming too absorbed (or perceived to be) into the formal child welfare system has to be carefully managed.

With regard to child care planning, it has been argued that there is a need to broaden our understanding of permanence and stability (see Moran, McGregor, & Devaney, 2017) to recognise the significance of relational permanence that mentoring can bring. For example, Greeson et al. (2015) have shown that many young people see the relational or emotional aspects of permanence as more important than the legal or physical, leading to a focus on the concept of 'relational permanence' as an additional way to conceptualise the meaning of permanence (Freundlich, Avery, Munson, & Gerstenzang, 2006). Relational permanence has been defined by Semanchin Jones and LaLiberte (2013, p. 509) as 'youth experiencing a sense of belonging through enduring life-long connections to parents, extended family or other caring adults, including at least one adult who will provide a permanent, parent-like connection for that youth'. Relationships with natural mentors where successful and occurring over time can be considered to be a form of relational permanence and these need to feature more within more traditional thinking about permanence and stability for children in care.

Prioritise friendship and empathic relationships in child welfare

Given that most mentoring programmes, no matter how well proven, are unlikely to be scalable to the extent that they will become universal 'standard issue' in child welfare, we need to explore how mainstream services can incorporate the helpful relational dynamics associated with mentoring into mainstream practice. Although in a different context of service users in palliative care services, research by Beresford, Adshead, and Croft (2007) showed that the demonstration of components of friendship by social workers towards the service users they worked with was not just seen as useful but an essential component of their intervention. Their research listed key sub-factors nominated by service users within the demonstration of friendship, and these were apart from the more obvious qualities of warmth and genuine interest in the client these included:

- Listening
- Being treated respectfully
- Being given time
- Being non-judgemental
- Being available and accessible

One could argue that this quality of 'friendship' in social work practice has lessened over time and needs reconsideration. Even allowing for the overriding statutory duty and responsibility of social workers which may be used as a reason, 'how' social workers relate with clients and do their work is as central as 'what' their intended outcome for their intervention might be. This is not to suggest that the role fundamentally changes to a mentoring role but that both the principles and practices of friendship building as reflected in mentoring are more mainstreamed into practice. This is particularly the case when it comes to direct work with children and young people. For example, research by O'Reilly and Dolan (2016) on child protection assessment has strongly demonstrated the value of 'friendly play' between social workers and young children as part of the assessment process.

For all adults involved in the lives of young people in care, including foster parents, social workers, residential care staff and mentors, the capacity to demonstrate their humanity through empathy with the young person can be seen as the fundamental gateway to a positive relationship. Empathy relates to the capacity not just to understand (as in this case) where a young person in or leaving care is experiencing (cognitive empathy) as well as identifying with his or her experience at an emotional level (affective empathy). Empathy can also be understood as an 'active concept' reflecting that adults have the power to go much further and be willing to act in the interests of the young person (Segal, 2011). The importance of ensuring empathic relational practice, at a system level, is of crucial importance given the evidence that lack of empathy or a perception of this lack from the individual worker to a young person can have profound impact on the individual feeling of support as well as long term negative impact on capacity to trust and engage in constructive helping relationships.

Address placement disruption, resourcing issues and staff turnover

Horn and Spencer (2018) highlight the barriers to the development of natural mentoring relationships that exist at the child welfare service level. Frequent disruption and changes of placement can mean that young people are moved from schools, neighbourhoods and communities where they have developed strong connections and possibly natural mentoring relationships which then become suspended. They argue that avoiding placement disruption can provide opportunities for youth to develop and maintain important relationships. Furthermore, Ahrens et al. (2011) also found that young people leaving care referred to relationships with adults they had met through the child welfare system as being of particular importance, indicating that this may be a particular source of support or 'natural mentors' for young people in care. Placement disruption is likely to undermine these relationships in the lives of young people.

Horn and Spencer (2018, p. 229) also highlight that a high turnover in staff in child welfare agencies can have a negative impact on the quality of relationships that are developed between these adults and children/young people, arguing 'because these relationships are models for how youth perceive relationships with other adults, more care should be taken in preventing unnecessary worker transition for youth in care'. The issue of social worker turnover was raised by young people in this study. In a context of high staff turnover, it is possible that social workers are likely to be inhibited from building a relationship that is akin to a friendship due to the risk that this cannot be sustained over time because their workload may change and the child may be re-allocated to another worker. One suggestion made by Moran et al. (2017) in practice guidance written with child care social work teams in Ireland was to have a system whereby changes of social worker were facilitated by a transitional period of joint working between the outgoing and incoming worker. Other practice supports would need to be developed to maximise the capacity for workers to balance between the limits of a professional relationship and the delivery of a relationship-based service to young people that is best if done through an informal, relaxed and trusting relationship. Furthermore, in order for workers to be able to invest the necessary time and resources to build and sustain meaningful relationships with the young person in care, significant investment of resources is needed within the system to enable this to happen. This ranges from the most basic of resources such as ability to take children out socially, pay for activities and outings to recognition of the need for ongoing training and support in use of play and recreation and the development of core youth work skills.

8.5 Practice implications for youth mentoring programmes and organisations

Drawing on learning across the volume, we now move on to identify a series of messages for youth mentoring organisations specifically in relation to youth mentoring for young people in care.

Adhere to evidence based practice guidelines: According to Stelter et al. (2017), there is growing evidence supporting the potential of mentoring for being an effective intervention to address the needs of and promote positive outcomes of youth in foster care. While it is acknowledged that there is a substantial gap in the literature regarding what intervention components contribute to the development of an enduring mentoring relationship and what practices aid programs in being most effective for this population of youth, it is widely accepted that the chances of successful outcomes are greater in programmes that adhere to best practice standards in terms of child protection, training, assessment, ongoing support and troubleshooting.[1] Mentoring relationships that are not carefully planned and managed can be harmful to young people. As Spencer et al. argue:

> Handling the intricate dynamics of vulnerable youths and their families is a profound challenge requiring a high degree of clinical skill. Introduction of a mentor into a youth's life might cause a parent to feel

threatened, a youth to feel conflicted, or a sibling to feel jealous, for example. No program would intend to create these feelings, and a good programme would be conscious of these possibilities and take actions to address them. They remain risks nonetheless.

(Spencer et al., 2010, p. 231)

Spencer et al. (2010) also warn that in a climate of limited resources, there is a risk that funding will be directed towards increasing the quantity of mentoring matches rather than focusing on the quality of a smaller number of matches. Given the potential to do harm in youth mentoring and the particular vulnerabilities associated with young people in care (highlighted earlier in this chapter), it is critical that a 'quality first' approach is taken. This involves robust investing in recruitment, assessment, training, matching, supervision and monitoring as well as providing resources for match activities.

Mentor characteristics and the importance of good matching: The characteristics of mentors identified by young people in this and previous studies as helpful include being easy-going, relaxed, non-judgemental, trustworthy, empathetic, honest and authentic. Mentors were also described as having a non-directive approach, supporting young people's agency and autonomy and encouraging them to make decisions for themselves. As noted earlier, children in care can sometimes feel powerless in the context of their own lives due to the fact that many decisions made are outside of their control (Jackson, Brady, Forkan, Tierney, & Kennan, 2018). When recruiting mentors to work with children in care, mentoring organisations should pay attention to these findings and prioritise mentors who adopt an autonomy supportive approach (Brumovska, 2017).

While good 'matching' or ensuring compatibility between mentor and mentee is important in all youth mentoring practice, its importance for children in care must be emphasised. Ahrens et al. (2011) argue that more attention should be paid to matching of foster care youth. In our study, young people frequently referred to the fact that they and their mentors shared similar interests, which made it much easier for companionship and a bond to develop. It also contributes to ensuring that a longer-term relationship is developed, because both parties derive enjoyment from mutually enjoyable activities. A useful example is that of Sean and his mentor, Stephen, whereby their shared love of squash means that they will continue to meet for weekly matches even after their mentoring relationship has formally ended.

Mentor background: Research has shown that one factor which may increase the success of a mentor match is the mentor having similar experiences to the young people in care (Britner & Collins, 2018). Kirk and Day (2011) studied a campus based programme for young people making the transition from foster care and found that young people were most inspired by mentors who had previous foster care experience, with the young participants reporting that they felt they could identify with and trust people who were similar to themselves more easily. Munson, Smalling, Spencer, Scott, and Tracy (2010) also argue that mentoring programmes should recruit adults that have had similar life experiences, particularly those that have had some experience of the care system. They speculate that having had similar difficult experiences may help to reduce shame and lead to young people 'bringing more of themselves into the relationships' (p. 533).

Furthermore, as we saw in Chapters 3 and 4, there is a growing body of evidence that youth mentoring relationships (both natural and formal) are more beneficial when the mentor has experience in helping roles or professions (Jarjoura, Tanyu, Forbush, Herrera, & Keller, 2018; Van Dam et al., 2018; Raposa, Erickson, Hagler, & Rhodes, 2018). In our study, some of the young people referred to their mentors having backgrounds in youth work, teaching or social care and their narratives suggest that in addition to friendship and emotional support, their mentors connected them with a range of opportunities and resources that were of benefit to them and advocated for them where needed. It is also possible that their mentoring relationship lasted longer because their mentors worked in this area. Mentors with specific training as helping professionals may have the skills to bond effectively with difficult and/or resistant youth. However, as noted in Chapter 7, this should not be interpreted as suggesting that mentors with other backgrounds were not successful but highlights that mentors with this profile may bring an additional skill set.

Support match longevity: Continuity and longevity in mentoring relationship is particularly important for young people in care. Research shows that the longer the relationship, the greater the likelihood of a positive outcome. As Clayden and Stein (2005) found, young people who were mentored for over a year were more likely to have achieved their original goals and have future plans. Young people participating in our research valued the long-term consistency and continuity of support available from their mentors. This was of particular value to young people making the transition to adulthood without the scaffolding of family support. Mentoring programmes working with young people in care should ensure that match longevity is supported as much as possible.

Need for advocacy in relation to the potential of mentoring: At a broad level, youth mentoring programmes and organisations have a leadership role to play in expanding the use of mentoring to support young people in care. The assumption that youth mentoring is really only useful as prevention to care placement is a basic myth which needs to be debunked both in policy and practice. As is shown in this book, the untapped potential for youth mentoring for young people in care and leaving care is significant. Youth mentoring organisations are well-positioned to provide leadership to statutory child welfare services to help build relationships at meso, exo and macro levels to open up greater scope for developing youth mentoring as a practice in formal child welfare practices and exploring how greater use of mentoring can be developed to support children in care. Mentoring programmes can be a 'gel' that not only links youth to mentors but professionals to each other in the best interest of the young person living in care.

Embrace new approaches to supporting mentoring: While youth mentoring organisations have traditionally supported formal mentoring whereby a young person is matched with an adult they did not previously know, they should reflect on opportunities offered by new models of youth mentoring that embrace the use of natural mentoring for children in care. It has been argued that youth mentoring organisations serving youth leaving foster care should look carefully at ways of strengthening existing natural mentoring relationships and supporting young people to develop high quality relationships in the transition to adulthood, rather than trying to create new ones (Horn and Spencer (2018); Greeson (2013); Munson et al. (2010). Likewise, Avery (2010) encourages practice models that rely on youth to identify significant adults in permanency plan development, while, Duke, Farruggia and Germo (2017) advocate for helping foster care youth find and build relationships with the non-parental adults in their lives.

Youth-initiated mentoring is an emerging approach where youth can select a natural network member as a mentor, be it a family member, neighbour, friend, youth worker and so on. What is key to this emergent approach and highlighted in Chapter 3 is the fact that it recognises, formalises and bolsters the naturally occurring support for the young person within his or her own communities (Spencer, Gowdy, Drew, & Rhodes, 2019). The added benefit of this approach is a greater likelihood of the match being sustainable and, because the young person selects, he or she is more likely to choose somebody who he or she respects and likes. While research on YIM in still in its infancy, it is an approach that mentoring organisations should consider.

8.6 Conclusion

We argue in this book that overall from the evidence produced, literature and other prior research considered and limited wisdom of the authors, mentoring for children and youth living in care is a good thing that brings personal benefits and real friendship to them and should be developed further. It has added value and despite risks, limitations and a caveat of needing to be of high quality rather than quantity, has a promising future. While there are challenges for professionals, most notably social workers and for care systems, these are not insurmountable but do require attention. Relationships emerge as the key ingredient not just in the mentor-mentee connection but also across the social ecology of the young person. New and innovative forms of mentoring will emerge for young people in care or leaving care. The practice and policy challenge just like the research challenge is not just to be part of that innovation but to help lead it. Ultimately that will be to the betterment of the care experience of young people who are the ones that truly matter.

Summary messages

- The significance of quality of relationships for young people in care is strongly evidenced in this book.
- Mentoring relationships can help young people in care are supported in their interactions between their often complex and multi-layered micro and meso system and the wider exo and macro systems.
- The views and experiences of young people in care reported in this book and from existing research need to be urgently responded to with regard to addressing system and practice approaches that continue to fail to recognise the importance of relationship based practice in this field.
- Even though social workers cannot befriend a young person beyond their professional role, there is much to be learnt from the ethos and principles of mentoring that can improve practice and supports provided.
- Changes within child welfare systems need to occur to allow the benefits of mentoring to be maximised ranging from individual supports to workers to do friendship and relationship based work to wider cultural change that shifts focus from overly proceduralised support for young people in care to relational oriented services.
- When developing informal and formal mentoring for children in care, the higher risks and challenges have to be recognised and appropriate support provided.

Note

1 For latest guidance, see MENTOR, The National Mentoring Partnership www.mentoring.org/program-resources/elements-of-effective-practice-for-mentoring/

References

Ahrens, K. R., Dubois, D. L., Garrison, M., Spencer, R., Richardson, L. P., & Lozano, P. (2011). Qualitative exploration of relationships with important non-parental adults in the lives of youth in foster care. *Children and Youth Services Review*, 33(6), 1012–1023.

Ahrens, K. R., Dubois, D. L., Richardson, L. P., Fan, M. Y., & Lozano, P. (2008). Youth in foster care with adult mentors during adolescence have improved adult outcomes. *Pediatrics*, 121(2), 246–252.

Avery, R. J. (2010). An examination of theory and promising practice for achieving permanency for teens before they age out of foster care. *Children and Youth Services Review*, 32(3), 399–408.

Beresford, P., Adshead, L., & Croft, S. (2007). *Palliative care, social work, and service users: Making life possible*. London: Jessica Kingsley Publishers.

Britner, P. A., & Collins, C. M. (2018). Permanent and formal connections. In E. Trejos-Castillo & N. Trevino-Schafer (Eds.), *Handbook of foster youth* (pp. 473–487). New York, NY: Routledge.

Bronfenbrenner, U. (1986). Ecology of the family as a context for human development: Research perspectives. *Developmental Psychology*, 22(6), 723–742.

Bronfenbrenner, U., & Crouter, A. C. (1983). The evolution of environ- mental models in developmental research. In W. Kessen (Ed.), His- torg, theorg, and methods, Volume 1 of P. H. Mussen (Ed.), *Handbook of child psychology* (4th ed., pp. 357–414). New York, NY: Wiley.

Bronfenbrenner, U., & Morris, P. A. (1998). The ecology of developmental processes. In W. Damon & R. M. Lerner (Ed.), *Handbook of child psychology: Vol. 1. Theoretical models of human development* (Vol. Ed., 5th ed., pp. 993–1028). New York, NY: Wiley.

Brumovska, T. (2017). *Initial motivation and its impact on quality and dynamics in formal youth mentoring relationships: A longitudinal qualitative study* (PhD thesis), National University of Ireland, Galway. Retrieved from https://aran.library.nuigalway.ie/handle/10379/7119

Clayden, J., & Stein, M. (2005). *Mentoring young people leaving care – 'Someone for me'*. York: The University of York and the Joseph Rowntree Foundation.

Connolly, M., & Masson, J. (2014). Private and public voices: Does family group conferencing privilege the voice of children and families in child welfare? *Journal of Social Welfare and Family Law*, 36(4), 403–414.

Dolan, P., & Brady, B. (2012). *A guide to youth mentoring: Providing effective social support*. London and Philadelphia, PA: Jessica Kingsley Publishers.

Duke, T., Farruggia, S. P., & Germo, G. R. (2017). "I don't know where I would be right now if it wasn't for them": Emancipated foster care youth and their important non-parental adults. *Children and Youth Services Review*, 76, 65–73.

Freundlich, M., Avery, R. J., Munson, S., & Gerstenzang, S. (2006). The meaning of permanency in child welfare: Multiple stakeholder perspectives. *Children and Youth Services Review*, 28(7), 741–760.

Golightley, M., & Holloway, M. (2018). The personal and professional: Towards a more holistic knowledge base. *British Journal of Social Work*, 48(1–7), 1831–1835.

Greeson, J. K. (2013). Foster youth and the transition to adulthood: The theoretical and conceptual basis for natural mentoring. *Emerging Adulthood*, 1(1), 40–51.

Greeson, J. K., Garcia, A. R., Kim, M., Thompson, A. E., & Courtney, M. E. (2015). Development & maintenance of social support among aged out foster youth who received independent living services: Results from the multi-site evaluation of foster youth programs. *Children and Youth Services Review*, 53, 1–9.

Hayes, N., O' Toole, L., & Halpenny, A. M. (2017). *Introducing Bronfenbrenner: A guide for practitioners and students in early years education (Introducing Early Years Thinkers)*. London: Routledge.

Horn, J. P., & Spencer, R. (2018). Natural mentoring to support the establishment of permanency for youth in foster care. *Handbook of foster youth* (p. 173). New York, NY: Routledge.

Hyslop, I. (2018). Neoliberalism and social work identity. *European Journal of Social Work*, 21(1), 20–31.

Jackson, R., Brady, B., Forkan, C., Tierney, E., & Kennan, D. (2018). *Collective participation of children in care: A formative evaluation of the Tusla/EPIC foster care action groups*. Galway: UNESCO Child and Family Research Centre, NUI Galway.

Jarjoura, G. R., Tanyu, M., Forbush, J., Herrera, C., & Keller, T. E. (2018). *Enhancement demonstration program: Technical report*. Washington, DC: American Institutes for Research.

Jones, A. S., & LaLiberte, T. (2013). Measuring youth connections: A component of relational permanence for foster youth. *Children and Youth Services Review*, 35(3), 509–517.

Kirk, R., & Day, A. (2011). Increasing college access for youth aging out of foster care: Evaluation of a summer camp program for foster youth transitioning from high school to college. *Children and Youth Services Review*, 33(7), 1173–1180.

McGregor, C. A. (2019). Paradigm framework for social work theory for early 21st century practice. *The British Journal of Social Work*, bcz006. Retrieved from https://doi.org/10.1093/bjsw/bcz006

Moran, L., McGregor, C., & Devaney, C. (2017). *Outcomes for permanence and stability for children in long-term care: Practice guidance*. Galway: UNESCO Child and Family Research Centre.

Munson, M. R., Smalling, S. E., Spencer, R., Scott, L. D., Jr., & Tracy, E. M. (2010). A steady presence in the midst of change: Non-kin natural mentors in the lives of older youth exiting foster care. *Children and Youth Services Review*, 32(4), 527–535.

O'Reilly, L., & Dolan, P. (2016). The voice of the child in social work assessments: Age-appropriate communication with children. *The British Journal of Social Work*, 46(5), 1191–1207.

Raposa, E. B., Erickson, L. D., Hagler, M., & Rhodes, J. E. (2018). How economic disadvantage affects the availability and nature of mentoring relationships during the transition to adulthood. *American Journal of Community Psychology*, 61(1–2), 191–203.

Segal, E. A. (2011). Social empathy: A model built on empathy, contextual understanding, and social responsibility that promotes social justice. *Journal of Social Service Research*, 37(3), 266–277.

Spencer, R., Collins, M. E., Ward, R., & Smashnaya, S. (2010). Mentoring for young people leaving foster care: Promise and potential pitfalls. *Social Work*, 55(3), 225–234.

Spencer, R., Gowdy, G., Drew, A. L., & Rhodes, J. E. (2019). "Who Knows Me the Best and Can Encourage Me the Most?": Matching and early relationship development in youth-initiated mentoring relationships with system-involved youth. *Journal of Adolescent Research*, 34(1), 3–29.

Stein, M. (2012). *Young people leaving care: Supporting pathways to adulthood*. London: Jessica Kingsley.

Stelter, R. L., Kupersmidt, J. B., & Stump, K. N. (2017). Supporting mentoring relationships of youth in foster care: Do program practices predict match length? *American Journal of Community Psychology*, 61(3–4), 398–410.

Thompson, A. E., Greeson, J. K. P., & Brunsink, A. M. (2016). Natural mentoring among older youth in and aging out of foster care: A systematic review. *Children and Youth Services Review*, 61, 40–50.

Van Dam, L., Smit, D., Wildschut, B., Branje, S. J. T., Rhodes, J. E., Assink, M., & Stams, G. J. J. M. (2018). Does natural mentoring matter? A multilevel meta-analysis on the association between natural mentoring and youth outcomes. *American Journal of Community Psychology*, 62(1–2), 203–220.

Index

adolescence: children and young people in care and 2–3; described 2
adolescents, challenges faced by 2
adoption for care, defined 26
Adshead, L. 141
Advocates to Successful Transition to Independence 68
Ahrens, K. R. 45, 48, 50, 51, 139–140, 142, 144
Albright, J. N. 64
alternative care 3; features for children in 28–29; formal, defined 26; permanence and stability themes in 36–37
Andersen, S. H. 29, 33
authenticity, mentoring relationships and 122

Baart, A. 130
Bailey-Etta, B. 33
Beresford, P. 141
Better Outcomes, Brighter Futures: The National Policy Framework for Children and Young People, 2014–2020 77–78
Big Brothers Big Sisters community mentoring programmes 63, 65; helpful features of 124–125; see also Foróige Big Brothers Big Sisters study
Big Brothers Big Sisters International 80
bonding social capital 15–16
Brady, B. 5, 36, 63, 130
Brady, E. 29
Braun, V. 86–87
bridging social capital 16
Briggs, E. C. 65
Brown, A. W. 33
Brown, J. 35
Brunsink, A. M. 45

Brustera, B. E. 68
Busse, H. 64

Cameron, C. 29
Campbell, R. 64
Canavan, J. 129
Cantwell, N. 37
Cappa, C. 26
care: definitions of 26–27; diversity of 27–29; future challenges of 37; and permanency planning, focus on mentoring in 51; stigma of being in 30–31; transitioning from, becoming independent and 34–35
care leavers 3–5
care period 27
Cassel, J. 11
Chapman, C. M. 60
Child Care Act 77
Child Care Law Reporting Project 79
child development 3
children and young people in care: at adolescence 2–3; in care, defined 3; ecological approach to 33–34, 35; formal mentoring for (see formal mentoring for children in care/leaving care); groups of 34–35; introduction to 1–5; and leaving care 3–5; mentoring for (see youth mentoring for young people in care); natural mentoring for 44–51; negative impacts of (see negative impacts, children in care); permanence/stability and 36–37; professional services impact on 35–36; social ecology model for 34–35; transition to adulthood and 34–35; youth mentoring for 8–9
children's participation, defined 83–84

child welfare systems: barriers to development in 142–143; friendship/empathic relationships in 141–142; guidance for 139–143; post-care mentoring value and support 140–141; relationships and, importance of 139–140; social work implications for 137–139; youth mentoring options for 140
civic engagement, youth mentoring and 105–106, 107
Clarke, V. 87
Clayden, J. 6, 9, 16, 67, 69, 145
Coccomaa, P. 68
cognitive development, mentor/mentee relationship and 10
Cohen, S. 12
Colley, H. 125
Commission to Inquire into Child Abuse 30
community-based mentoring 7
Connolly, M. 29
Connolly, N. 35
context component of ecological context 135
continuity, mentoring relationships and 122
Cooley, C. H. 10, 109
coping: defined 13; resilience of children and 30; youth mentoring and 13–14
Courtney, M. G. 60
Coyle, D. 34
Craig, T. K. J. 69
Croft, S. 141
Culhane, S. E. 67
Curtin, C. 63
Cutrona, C. E. 125

Davidson, J. C. 37
Day, A. 68, 144
Day, C. 36
Deane, K. L. 60
deinstitutionalisation 27
del Valle, J. F. 28
Deutsch, N. L. 120
Devaney, C. 33, 35
De Wit, D. J. 60, 81
Dinisman, T. 35
diversity of care 27–29
Dolan, P. 81, 130, 142
Donlan, A. E. 122
door openers, described 16

Drew, A. L. 53
DuBois, D. 45, 60–62, 66, 81
Duke, T. 16, 46, 146
Dweck, C. S. 115

Eccles, J. S. 2
ecological context: components of 135–136; dual identity and systems in 33–34
educational engagement, progression and 101–104, 114–115
Elsley, S. 37
emotional support, youth mentoring and 95–97, 114
emotional well-being, youth mentoring and 93–94
emotions, understanding and dealing with 97–98, 113
empathy, mentoring relationships and 121–122, 142
Erdem, G. 81
Erickson, E. H. 2, 10, 109
experiential empathy 122

Fahlberg, V. 37
family based care, other forms of 26
Fan, M. Y. 45
Farmer, E. 30
Farruggia, S. P. 46, 146
Fisher, J. 81
formal alternative care: defined 26; types of 26; UN Guidelines on 27
formal mentoring: described 6; forms of 8–9; programs, described 1, 6
formal mentoring for children in care/leaving care: challenges/limitations associated with 62–65; general mentoring programmes for 65–66; intensive mentoring models for 66–67; introduction to 59; mentoring projects for young people leaving care 67–68; positive outcomes in 61–62; practice considerations and challenges in 69–70; research evidence in relation to 59–62; research on 65–68; SAYes example 68
Foróige Big Brothers Big Sisters study: child welfare in Ireland and 77–79; data analysis 86–87; ethical considerations for 85–86; interviews 86; introduction to 77; overview 83–87; rationale for 81–83; research

Index

advisory group 83–84; research participants, profile of 87–88; sampling/recruitment for 84; setting for 79–81
foster care 3; defined 26
Foster Forward 52
Freud, S. 10
Frydenberg, E. 13, 113–115

Gardner, F. 33, 114
Garmezy, N. 44
Gelis, J. F. 61, 64–65, 115
Germo, G. R. 46, 146
Giller, H. 44
Gilligan, R. 29, 31, 78
Goodloe, C. L. 120
Gootman, J. A. 2
Gowdy, G. 53
Greeson, J. K. 51, 141, 146
Greeson, J. K. P. 43, 45, 49–50, 51
Gross, P. 26
Grossman, J. B. 11, 44, 62–63, 65
Grotberg, E. 14
group care, defined 26
Gypen, L. 32

Haight, W. L. 65
Harré, N. 60
Harris, T. O. 69
Hendry, L. B. 64
Herrera, C. 66, 69
Hines, A. M. 68
honesty, mentoring relationships and 122
Horn, J. P. 49, 51–52, 54, 142, 146
Hubbard, K. 69
Hurd, N. M. 64
Hussain, S. B. 64

identity development, mentor/mentee relationship and 10, 11, 107–112, 116
in care 3–4; defined 3; types of 3
individual supervised care, defined 26
informal: care outside kinship care 27; kinship care 3, 27
informal mentors 5
institutional care, defined 26
interests, matching based on similar 61
Ireland, child welfare in 77–79; *see also* Foróige Big Brothers Big Sisters study

Johnson, H. E. 120
Johnson, S. B. 8, 65, 66

Jones, A. S. 51, 141
Jordan, J. V. 15

Keller, T. E. 62, 124
Kennan, D. 82
Kennedy Report 82
Khoo, E. 34, 128
kinship care, defined 26
Kipping, R. 64
Kiraly, M. 29
Kirk, R. 68, 144
Köngeter, S. 35
Krauss, S. M. 16
Kupersmidt, J. B. 66, 140

LaLiberte, T. 51, 141
Larose, S. 81
Larsson, B. 30
Lehmann, J. 33, 114
Leinster, J. 37
Lester, A. M. 120, 122
Lewis, J. 83
Liang, B. 64, 115
life course trajectories, children in care 29–30
lifelines, described 16
life story work 31–32
Lipman, E. L. 81
listening, youth mentoring and 95–97
long term care, defined 27
López, M. 28
Lozano, P. 45
Lynch, M. 5, 36

MacDonald, R. 16
Mangold, K. 35
Markward, M. 130
Markward, N. 130
Martinovich, Z. 8, 65
Masten, A. 14, 112
McCrae, L. 29
McGregor, C. 5, 33, 35, 36
McKenzie, V. 13
McMillan, L. 130
McMillen, J. C. 46
Mead, G. H. 10, 109
Mendis, K. 33, 114
mentee as Little Brother or Sister 80
mentoring *see* youth mentoring
mentoring relationships 120; aim of 6; authenticity and 122; continuity and 122–123; empathy and 121–122; honesty and 122; mentee decision

making and 123; natural (*see* natural mentoring relationships); pathways of influence 9–10; trust and 121
mentors: backgrounds of 62, 147; as the Big Brother or Sister 81; characteristics, good matching and 144; defined 5; as external regulators 44; helpful characteristics/relational qualities of 119–123; as institutional agents 44; match longevity and 145; and mentees, frequency of meetings 61; styles used by 62; training for 51, 61–62
Mertz, M. 29
Michelson, D. 36
Miller, J. B. 15, 116
Milligan, I. 37
mindset concept 115
Mitchell, G. 29
Moodie, M. L. 81
Moore, J. 60
Moran, L. 33, 36, 37, 143
Munson, M. R. 46, 47, 49, 50, 51, 145, 146

Nandy, S. 27
narrative research, described 83
National Longitudinal Study of Adolescent Health 45
natural mentor: characteristics of 50; defined 44; key feature of 47
natural mentoring 1; challenges in forming/maintaining relationships 49; for children in care 44–51; examples 6; introduction to 43; outcomes of 45–47; overview of 43–44; prevalence of 45–47; relationships, characteristics of positive 47–48; research on, implications for practice from 49–51; as social policy intervention 1; studies on 43–44
natural mentoring relationships: care/permanency planning, mentoring in 51; characteristics of positive 47–48; mentor recruitment and 50; research on 49–51; supporting development of 49–50; support youth to identify mentors 50; training for mentors 51
navigators, described 16
negative impacts, children in care: care definitions 26–27; coping, resilience and 30; diversity of care and 27–29; ecological context, dual identity/systems and 33–34; future challenges for 37; health, education and well-being outcomes 32–33; introduction to 25; life course trajectories and 29–30; permanence and stability themes 36–37; pre-care experiences, impact of 31–32; professional services involvement 35–36; stigma of being in care 30–31; transition to adulthood and 34–35
Newton, J. A. 69
Nicholls, C. M. 83
Nightingale Project 61
non-productive coping strategies 113, 114, 115
Nygren, L. 34, 128

Ocean, M. 52
O'Reilly, L. 142
Ormston, R. 83
Osterling, K. L. 68

Parks, S. H. 11
permanence: and care planning, focus on mentoring in 51; children in alternative care and 36–37; relational 51, 141
person component of ecological context 135–136
Petrowski, N. 26
Philip, K. 60, 64, 65, 125
Pilisuk, M. 11
Pinkerton, J. 34
Portillo, N. 61
positive natural mentoring relationships, characteristics of 47–48
pre-care experiences, impact of 31–32
Preston, J. M. 6
Prieto-Flores, Ò. 64–65, 115
Princes Trust and Camelot Foundation 67
process component of ecological context 135
productive coping 113–115
professional services, impact of 35–36
protective factors 14
Pryce, J. M. 8, 12, 65, 66

qualitative methods, described 83
Quinn, N. 37

Raposa, E. B. 61
Rappaport, N. 64, 115

Index

Refaeli, T. 35
Reimer, D. 29
Reissmann, C. 83
relational connections, key outcomes from 15
relational cultural theory (RCT) 14–15, 115, 128, 136
relational dynamics, youth perspectives on: BBBS programme and 124–125; introduction to 119; mentors, characteristics/qualities of 119–123; young person's social network, mentor role in 125–128
relational mentoring 15
relational permanence 51, 141
relational resilience 15
relationships: close and trusting 61; as 'the match' 81
Report of the Commission to Inquire into Child Abuse (Ryan Report) 79
Resch, N. L. 11
residential care 3; defined 26
resilience: of children, coping and 30; described 14; youth mentoring and 13–14
Rhodes, J. E. 9–11, 44, 52, 53, 61, 62, 65, 109
Richardson, L. P. 45
Ritchie, J. 83
Roarty, N. 37
Robberechts, M. 31
Rock, S. 36
Roffman, J. 44
Rogers, J. 31
Rutter, M. 44
Ryan Report 82

Samuels, G. M. 12
Satka, M. 35
SAYes 68
Schofield, G. 30, 109, 113, 116
Schwartz, S. E. 52
Scott, L. D., Jr. 47, 145
secure/special care, defined 26
Seden, J. 3
self-confidence, building 98–100
Selwyn, J. 27
Serbinski, S. 35
shared relational excitement 120
Shildrick, T. 16
Silverthorn, N. 61
Simpson, H. 28
Singer, E. R. 12
Skoog, V. 34, 128

Smalling, S. E. 47, 145
Smith, M. 29
Smith, S. 43
sociability, building 98–100
social capital: bonding 16; bridging 16; described 16; types of 16
social capital, youth mentoring and 16–17, 104–105, 107, 115
social development, mentor/mentee relationship and 10
social justice, youth mentoring and 64–65
social network, mentor role in young person's 125–128
social outlet, youth mentoring and 94–95
social support: defined 11; youth mentoring and 11–12
social well-being, youth mentoring and 93–94
social work: child welfare systems and 137–139; neo-liberalism impact on 138; relationships and 138
Southwick, S. M. 44
special care, defined 26
Spencer, R. 47, 49, 51–54, 63, 64, 65, 69, 115, 122, 142, 143, 144, 145, 146
Spina, S. U. 44
Spratt, J. 60, 65
stability, children in alternative care and 36–37
Stack, N. 35
Stanton-Salazar, R. D. 44
Steels, S. 28
Stein, M. 6, 7, 8, 16, 32, 67, 69, 145
Stelter, R. L. 66, 69, 140, 143
Stroobants, T. 31
Stump, K. N. 66, 140
Sulimani-Aidan, Y. 35, 113, 115
Sutton, L. 35

Taussig, H. N. 67
Thematic Analysis (TA) 86
Thompson, A. E. 43, 45
Thomson, S. 36
time component of ecological context 135
Tracy, E. M. 47, 145
transitions 2; identity and 107–112, 116
trust, mentoring relationships and 121
Tugenberg, T. 52
Tusla (Irish national Child and Family Agency) 78–79

UN Convention on the Rights of the Child (UNCRC) 77, 81–82
UN Guidelines on Alternative Care 26, 37

Valentine, J. C. 61
Van Dam, L. 44, 52–53
Vanderfaeillie, J. 31
Van Holen, F. 31
Vanschoonlandt, F. 31
very important nonparental adults (VIPs) 46

Walker, G. 64
Ward, E. 30
Wenger, R. S. 43
Werner, E. E. 43
West, J. 64, 115
White, L. 35
Wills, T. A. 12
Winter, K. 34

Yeager, D. S. 115
young people in care *see* children and young people in care
youth-initiated mentoring 7–8; benefits associated with 53–54; challenges associated with 54; components of 51–52; goal of 51–52; introduction to 43; overview of 51–52; practice example of 52–53; web resources for 54
youth mentoring: benefits of (*see* youth mentoring, benefits of); for children in care 8–9 (*see also* youth mentoring for young people in care); coping and 13; described 5; growth in, United States and worldwide 6; history of 5; influence, pathways of 9–10; issues/challenges associated with 8–9; overview of 5–7; programs, described 1; relational cultural theory of 14–15; resilience and 13–14; Rhodes model of 9–11; social capital and 15–16; social justice and 64–65; social support and 11–12
youth mentoring, benefits of: civic engagement and 104–105, 107; educational engagement, progression and 101–104, 114–115; emotional support, listening and 94–95, 114; emotions, understanding and dealing with 97–98, 114; introduction to 93; 'like family' mentoring relationships 100–101, 114; mindset concept and 115–116; resilience and 112–113; self-confidence/sociability, building 98–100; social capital and 104–105, 108, 115; social/emotional well-being and 93–94; social outlet, providing 94–95; transitions, identity and 107–112, 116
youth mentoring for young people in care: child welfare practice, guidelines for 139–143; child welfare regimes and 137–139; introduction to 135; programmes/organisations, practice implications for 143–146; value of 135–137
youth mentoring programmes/organisations, practice implications for 143–146; advocacy for mentoring potential 145–146; evidence-based guidelines 143–144; match longevity and 145; mentor background 144–145; mentor characteristics, good matching and 144; mentoring support, new approaches to 146

Zeira, A. 35
Zinn, A. 46, 50